July 2003

For Matthew,

It wouldn't have looked anywhere near as good as it does without your help. Many thanks,

Mike.

G000272673

THE CHOICE
OF
CHAMPIONS

DAVID SUTTON

THE CHOICE OF CHAMPIONS

DAVID SUTTON

Foreword by Hannu Mikkola

LiveWire
Books

Copyright David Sutton 2003

All right reserved. No part of this publication may be reproduced or stored in a retrieval system or transmitted in any form or by any means, electronic, mechanical, photocopying or otherwise without the prior written permission of the publisher.

First published in 2003 for Historic Motorsport Limited by
Live Wire Books,
The Orchard,
School Lane,
Warmington,
Banbury,
OX17 1DE
Tel: 01295 690624

The right of David Sutton to be identified as the author of this work has been asserted in accordance with the Copyright, Designs and Patents Act 1988.

ISBN No. 0 9542860-1-4

A catalogue record for this book is available from the British Library.

Designed by Gemini Designs

Printed and bound in Great Britain by
Butler & Tanner Limited, Frome and London

DEDICATION

For Jill, who has stood steadfastly by my side for 36 years.

For my mother, Dorothy, who was my greatest fan and
who always believed in what I was doing.

For Guy, who will always be missed.

And for Ana and Ignacio, who gave me a new life in 1992.

CONTENTS

ACKNOWLEDGEMENTS

No book that spans nearly four decades of World Rallying could be written without regular reference to Martin Holmes' 25-year series of World Rallying annuals. Photographs have been generously donated by Martin Holmes, Reinhard Klein, Jim Adams, David Nicholson and many other friends. I am also indebted to Pauline Thomas for her tireless patience in endlessly re-typing the manuscript and to Michael Cable and Jill Todd of Live Wire Books for helping to put it all together. Finally, my thanks also to Audi UK for their support.

FOREWORD

I first met David Sutton in 1967, when he made a lasting impression on me by promising my friend Timo Mäkinen a rally car for that year's RAC Rally despite the fact that he didn't actually have a car at his disposal at the time or any type of budget with which to run the entry. He simply thought that if he had the services of the best driver in the world, everything else would take care of itself! And so it did. What's more, he and Timo very nearly won the event.

This illustrates David's character perfectly. He is always ready to put everything at stake when it comes to motorsport and to take the risks necessary to achieve top results. He is also skilled at keeping the best people around him. I have driven many events for him over the years and, without fail, his cars have always been prepared to the very highest standard.

Above all, he is a survivor. I have never met anyone quite like him when it comes to keeping an optimistic outlook through both good times and bad. Faced with the sort of setbacks in recent years that might have overwhelmed a lesser man, he has found the strength to get back on his feet. For that, he has my great admiration.

He and Jill are loving godparents to my eldest son, Juha, and the whole Mikkola family is proud to count them among our oldest and dearest friends. I would like to thank Jill for the hospitality that she has shown us countless times over the years.

And David - thank you for everything in the last thirty-five years. I wish you the greatest success with your book and with your future.

HANNU MIKKOLA
Helsinki. May 2003

SUTTON & SONS

It was love at first sight. I was eighteen years old and had just started a new job on the service reception desk at a Volkswagen dealership in my hometown of Nottingham when a particularly eye-catching silver Beetle suddenly drew up outside. Apart from the crackle of a highly tuned engine, what immediately excited my attention was the impressive array of spotlights strung across the front bumper bar and the searchlight mounted on the roof. I had never seen anything quite like it before.

Sauntering outside to take a closer look, I peered through the driver's side window to be confronted by a range of unfamiliar counters, dials and instruments, all of which looked extremely businesslike. I was intrigued. "What sort of car is this?" I asked the owner. Jim Adams was a highly successful young Midlands market trader, only about four years older than me. He explained that it was a Rally car and then proceeded, with great enthusiasm, to point out some of its more interesting features. These included a pair of what were then must-have Lucas SLR 700 spotlights, known as 'flame throwers', not to mention such mysterious state-of-the-art inboard gadgetry as a Halda Speed Pilot and Halda Tripmaster. It was spellbinding. I didn't fully realise it at the time, but, looking back, I think I can pinpoint this as the precise moment when my future was decided.

Given my family background, I suppose I had always been destined for a career somewhere in the motor industry or the transport business, although possibly in a rather more mundane capacity than that in which I was eventually to make my name. My parents, Leslie and Dorothy, were both working for Ford at

Dagenham when they met, my father as a truck driver and my mother in the trim department. However, by the time I was born on January 30th, 1940, the eldest of four brothers and one sister, the war had already turned their lives upside down. My mother had been switched to a war supply production line, where her function was to put the soft filler into soldier's helmets, while my father was allocated the rather unusual duty of driving a flatbed truck around the country with an anti-aircraft gun mounted on the back.

The idea behind this Dad's Army-style arrangement was that whenever advance warning was received of a bombing raid on a particular target in the region, Sutton Snr would be urgently dispatched with his mobile ack-ack to bolster the local defences. As it happened, he would probably have been more usefully employed staying put at home, since our own house, being located perilously close to the RAF base at Hornchurch, Essex, seemed to be under constant attack by the Luftwaffe. It was after the roof had been blown off for about the eleventh time that we were finally evacuated to Nottingham when I was about three years old.

As soon as the war was over my father decided to start his own small haulage business, successfully building it up from a one-truck, owner-driver operation to the point where he had over forty lorries on the road, only then to suffer a major setback when all road transport was nationalised under the post-war Labour government. Later, he re-launched the company as S&S Transport, S&S standing for Sutton and Sons.

Les Sutton was not the easiest man to get on with. A typically blunt Yorkshireman and a rugged individualist, he was one of a family of eight children, all of whom had all been brought up as Salvationists. A couple of my uncles actually went on to become senior officers in the Sally Army and although my father was something of a black sheep in this respect - rarely, if ever, setting foot inside a church himself - he insisted that his own children should keep the faith.

From an early age we had religion crammed down our throats. We had to go to church three times on Sundays and to choir and band practice twice during the week. Like all Salvationists, we were compulsorily required to learn how to play at least one musical instrument – and I chose the trumpet. I can still get a note or two out of the thing, although I have to admit that, even at my best, I was no Louis Armstrong. I did, however, have quite a good voice and was quickly co-opted into the choir.

Whenever they want to take the Mickey out of me, my family still love to dig out the faded snap that was taken of me in classic choirboy pose, dressed in a surplice, hymn book in hand. For my surprise 60th birthday party they had the photograph blown up to life size and made into a cardboard cut-out so that all the guests could have a good laugh while at the same time expressing amazement that I could ever once have looked so angelic.

Although I had passed the 11+, thereby qualifying for a Grammar School education, I actually spent nearly every spare moment in the evenings and at weekends down at the S&S depot, neglecting my homework in favour of messing about in the workshop, where I helped the mechanics to maintain and service the trucks. As a result, I left school at 16 with no 'O' levels to my name but with an ability to strip an engine down and rebuild it with my eyes shut. I duly joined the family firm and, as soon as I was old enough to get a licence, started driving the trucks around the country, occasionally venturing as far afield as Dounreay in Scotland where we had a contract with the power Station. My wages were £3-a-week.

Had it not been for my father's lack of financial savvy – and the crooked accountant whom he brought in to help him look after the books with even more disastrous results! – I suppose I might eventually have inherited a thriving business and could well have ended up trying to give Eddie Stobart and Norbert Destressangle a run for their money on the motorways of Europe instead of racing around the gravel roads and forest tracks of the world with the likes of Hannu, Ari, Timo, Markku and the rest.

As it was, the accountant set about embezzling thousands of pounds from S&S, helping to bring the company to its knees – a crime for which he duly went to prison amid a blaze of local publicity. While my father then retired to the pub to drown his sorrows, my mother decided it was time I found myself a proper job.

After scouring the 'Situations Vacant' columns of all the local newspapers in the area, she eventually spotted an ad placed by Beardall Motors, a local Volkswagen dealership in the nearby Nottingham suburb of West Bridgford, where they were looking for "a bright young man" to work in the service department.

Mum even took it upon herself to arrange an interview for me, at the end of which I could hardly believe my ears when George Beardall not only offered me the job but also named a starting salary of no less than £6-a-week – a princely sum in those days. And so it came about that in December 1958, smartly dressed in a crisp white shirt and my best Sunday suit, I turned up for work on what was to be the first day of the rest of my life.

Inspired by Jim Adams' eye-opening visit with his Rally car, it wasn't long before I started to take an active interest in the local Volkswagen Owners Club, getting my first taste of motorsport through the treasure hunts and driving tests that they organised. Nearly all rallying in those days was at this low-key club level, with the keener and more experienced members graduating to the sort of 150-mile Saturday night stuff where the emphasis was still very much on navigation. He who never misses his turnings, wins – that was the general rule at a time when the actual driving was relatively sedate compared with today. Most of those taking part in these club events would be using the same car that they would drive to work in on the Monday morning.

Although national and international rallies had been springing up all over Europe in the fifties, the image of the sport remained one of well-heeled Hooray Henrys driving their sports cars down to Monte Carlo, while less well off amateur enthusiasts hammered around country lanes in souped up family saloons. It wasn't until 1961 that the RAC, taking a leaf out of the Scandinavian book, developed the idea of special stage events on forest tracks. Then, in 1963, they created the first World Cup for manufacturers. This was based on five events, the Liege-Sofia-Liege Marathon de la Route, the Swedish Rally to the Midnight Sun, the Canadian Shell 4000, the East African Safari and the RAC Rally itself.

I went to see my first RAC that year and it came as another complete revelation as I got a thrilling first glimpse of the original Flying Finn, Timo Mäkinen, the great Roger Clark, Vic Elford, David Seigle-Morris and the other top drivers of the day in action in their Works Healeys, Cortinas and Mini Coopers. I remember coming away in a high state of excitement, thinking to myself: 'I've got to have a go at that one day'.

Back at Beardall's, meanwhile, I had rapidly graduated from junior service receptionist to salesman and had been presented with a brand new Beetle as my company car. In those days we used to carry out quite a few home demonstrations and one evening, returning very late after visiting a customer who lived some way out of Nottingham, I decided that in order to save my mother from going to the bother of cooking a meal for me, as she usually did, I would call in at the local fish and chip shop for a takeaway.

As I walked into the shop the woman behind the counter gave me a rather strange look and said sympathetically: "I'm so sorry to hear the bad news."

"What bad news?" I replied, caught completely by surprise.

"Oh, my God," she gasped, her hand going to her mouth. "Have you not been home yet?" With a rising sense of foreboding I explained that I was actually on my way at that moment, whereupon she blurted out that my father had suddenly dropped dead in the pub across the road earlier that evening.

I dashed back to find the family in a state of considerable and quite understandable disarray. It turned out that Les had collapsed and died of a massive heart attack while enjoying a couple of pints with his mates. Always a fairly heavy drinker, he had spent more and more of his time propping up the bar following the failure of his business, but there had been absolutely no warning of what was to come. He was only 52 when he died and, at 22, I found myself head of a household that by this time included my teenage sister Lynda and brothers Jeffrey, 20, Philip, 18 and three-year-old Stuart.

In these difficult circumstances, I was grateful for the fact that things were continuing to go well for me at Beardall's, where I had already made quite a name for myself as a salesman. One of those whom I had somehow managed to impress was Jim Adams. A regular customer by now, Jim would get me to give him a lift back to his home in Mansfield whenever he dropped off one of his cars or vans for servicing, a favour for which he would always reward me with a handsome tip of ten shillings, or even, sometimes, £1 – more than enough in those days to pay for a night out with my then girlfriend, Jean.

It nevertheless came as a complete surprise when he rang me out of the blue one day to request a private meeting, away from the office, at which he revealed that he had decided to branch out into the motor trade himself, with the purchase of a garage in Mansfield, and that he would like me to come and help him run it as Sales Manager. Totally taken aback, my first reaction was to tell him that I was actually very happy where I was. As a matter of courtesy, however, I agreed to go and have a look at the premises before finally making up my mind.

The set-up at Dukeries Garage, named after the area of Mansfield in which it was located, was very impressive and included a magnificent twenty-two-car showroom. As Jim showed me round it didn't take long for me to realise that this was an opportunity far too good to miss. Staying with Beardall's, a long-established and highly respected name in the area, would undoubtedly be the safer option. But at Dukeries I was being handed the chance of a lifetime to fast track myself into a senior management position in the motor trade at the age of just 22.

The clinching factor was the fabulous, award-winning apartment above the showroom that went with the job. Jean, to whom I was engaged by this time, was quick to point out that with a ready-made home like that to move into there was no reason why we couldn't get married straightaway. So that was that, of course! I gratefully accepted Jim's offer, gave my notice in at Beardall's and moved to Mansfield.

One of my first official duties in my new job was to join the Dukeries Motor Club and I soon found myself up to my neck in rally cars. Both Jim and the chief mechanic, George Morris, were great enthusiasts and, with all their friends from the Motor Club using the garage on a regular basis to service and upgrade their cars, we soon became established as one of the leading rally centres in the region.

It was all great fun in those days, with improvisation very much the name of the game when it came to preparing the cars. I remember sump shields being fashioned from off-cuts of what was allegedly the aluminium decking used in nuclear submarines, salvaged from a local engineering company whose owner happened to be a Club member, while Jim, famously, fitted his Triumph Vitesse with extra-wide wheels from an Atlas van.

I would look on in fascination as he and George and the rest of them spent all of Saturday tuning and polishing their cars, which I would then find on the forecourt early the next morning covered in thick mud and occasionally full of dents. As it happens, Jim, in particular, was a very talented driver who, I suspect, could easily have gone on to rival the likes of Roger Clark if he had been able to devote himself to motorsport full time. He was certainly quite a big name in club Rallying, his greatest claim to fame being that he once recorded the fastest times over a couple of stages of the Welsh Rally when the competition included Ove Anderssen.

The next big stage in my own rally driving education came when Jim had to drop out of a local East Midlands event at the last moment and invited me to take over the entry, in his car and with his regular co-driver Ray Palmer. Up until this point I had still not driven in anything more demanding than the odd club treasure hunt or autocross event so it was with a certain amount of apprehension that I climbed behind the wheel of Jim's prized Mini Cooper and set off on my first night rally.

It took a while for me to gain enough confidence in the dark to drive flat out on the wrong side of the road whenever my co-driver told me to do so, but I gradually began to get the hang of it and, before the night was out, I was actually starting to enjoy it – so much so that I didn't want to stop. When, on top of that, it was then announced that we had somehow managed to come 3rd overall I was hooked – even though this rather flattering result was more down to beginner's luck and my co-driver's expert navigation than any great driving skill on my part. Never mind. Absolutely exhausted, I was also almost deliriously elated. I'd definitely caught the bug.

Fired with this new enthusiasm I went out and bought myself a new Beetle, which was to be my rally car for the next year or so. With a selection of navigators, including Ray Palmer's son Geoff, I drove in a variety of events, spending my Saturday nights from 10pm until 4am roaring around deserted roads in some of the more remote parts of the East Midlands, the Yorkshire Dales and – a favourite location in those days – the Peak District in Derbyshire.

At other times, when we weren't rallying ourselves, Jim and I would occasionally go off for the weekend to watch the big boys in action in the Scottish, the Welsh and the RAC. I also remember going up to Barnby Moor to watch the Monte Carlo Rally come through on its way down from Scotland and being seized with the ambition to take part in an International event myself one day.

Then, just as I was starting to get into rallying in a big way, Jim ran into slight financial difficulties and Dukeries Garage was taken over by Central Motors in Mansfield. This proved to be a temporary arrangement and Jim was subsequently able to buy the business back,continuing to run it until quite recently. In the meantime, not being entirely sure where the takeover would leave me, I decided I had better sell my Volkswagen just in case I suddenly found myself out of a job and needed the money. As it turned out, I had nothing to worry about.

The new boss, Frank Mawer, was someone I had known since I was at Beardall's and he had actually tried once or twice to get me to go and work for him. "Always got a job for you, David my lad," he would say with a nod and a wink. There was even a story doing the rounds that he only bought Dukeries because I came with it. My position was therefore pretty secure.

What's more, I was able to talk him into letting me have my pick of any car in the showroom to use for weekend rallying, on condition that I didn't take it out of the showroom until we closed at 5.00pm on Saturday and that I made sure it was back in place in presentable condition by the time we opened again at 10.00am on Sunday. That gave me two or three hours on Saturday evening to get it ready, service it, change the tyres, bolt on the spotlights and install the map light and the same kind of time early on Sunday morning to reverse the process, clean it up and get it back on display. I had a little instant conversion kit and I got quite good at preparing any model in the time available.

It was around this time that I was instructed by Frank one day to arrange the collection of five second-hand cars that he had purchased from another dealer in Nottingham. I duly arrived there with a selection of drivers to ferry them back to Mansfield and, quite by chance, it turned out that I had been allocated a Cortina GT, one of the distinctive early models with the rev counter located on a binnacle on the steering column. As soon as we got out on the open road and I put my foot down I realised that it had all the makings of a brilliant rally car and I have to confess that when I got it back to Dukeries I stuck it right at the back of the showroom and made absolutely no attempt whatsoever to sell it, just so that I would be able to keep using it myself.

I proceeded to drive it with some success in a number of East Midlands events until eventually the suspension began to get a bit "soggy". I had no idea how to rectify this problem until a friend happened to mention that Ford had a Competition Department, operating from a disused airfield at Boreham, in Essex, where they offered a while-you-wait front suspension up-rating service for just £3.10.0d. Their tariff also included J wheels for £2.10.0 and a sump guard for £12. As soon as I could, I took a day off and drove down there in a borrowed Mini Cooper with the suspension struts in the boot and £3.10.0d in my pocket. It was a visit that marked another key turning point in my life.

Back in the early sixties security was nothing like as strict as it is nowadays and customers were free to browse around the workshops, where the cars were being prepared for Ford's own Rally programme. I took full advantage of this and, among other things, was dismayed to see mechanics cutting up and scrapping perfectly good cars that had been used either for actual events, testing or other development purposes.

After I had been down there several times and had got to know everybody quite well, I approached Bill Barnett, who was then Rally Manager, and asked if it would be possible to buy one of the ex-Works models that were strewn around in the huge yard at the back of the building in varying states of disrepair. The answer was an emphatic: "No!" I was told that in the whole history of the Ford Competition Department nobody had ever been allowed to buy a Factory rally car, the main reason being the worry that these vehicles often featured prototype components that might meanwhile have been withdrawn without ever becoming available to the general public.

Nevertheless, I refused to give up. One particular car that had caught my eye was a Lotus Cortina that I happened to notice had been lying in a corner of the yard for months, unused and unloved. It had been driven in the Tour de France by Vic Elford and David Seigle-Morris and was fitted with the traditional BRM-tuned Lotus twin cam engine.I pestered Bill endlessly and eventually got him to promise that he would at least talk to his superiors to see if there was any chance that they might make an exception and sell it to me. I didn't really hold out much hope, so you can imagine my delight when Bill called me out of the blue a few weeks later to say that it had been decided that I could have it after all and that the price would be £400.

The only problem was that although £400 may sound like nothing now, it was still a considerable amount in those days and I barely had 400 pennies to my name, let along £400. In the end, I managed to obtain the registration and chassis numbers from Bill, on the pretext that I needed them for insurance purposes. Armed with this information, I was then able to go to my local finance company and raise the money on a hire purchase agreement.

History was made on the day that I became the first person ever to buy an ex-Works Ford Rally car. In the years that followed I went on to buy more of them from Ford than any other person in the world, a fact that was confirmed when motorsport historian Graham Robson traced the registration numbers of every single Factory car ever sold and published the list in his book Works Escorts. But it is that first one that will stick forever in my memory.

As soon as I got it back to Mansfield I hurriedly re-sprayed it in Monaco Red and a few weeks later I realised another ambition when I drove it in the Scottish Rally – my first-ever International event in the first-ever privately owned ex-works Ford, a memorable double first as far as I was concerned. Partly for that very nostalgic reason, the Scottish Rally has always been one of my favourite events, despite the fact that on that debut occasion I had a few problems and didn't get a very good result.

It was at around this time that I actually managed to beat the late, great Roger Clark. This was pure fluke, of course, and not at all the heroic achievement that I nonchalantly make it out to be. The Dukeries Rally was an important round of the East Midlands Rally Championship in those days and, on this particular occasion, a large number of competitors, including Roger and his co-driver, Jim Porter, all contrived to make the same mistake at one of the early time controls. Managing to avoid this error myself, I came 23rd overall and could hardly believe my ears when I heard that Roger had finished behind me in 27th place.

I should add that I would have been even more amazed if you had told me then that this legendary figure, by far the best British driver of his day and perhaps of all time, would one day be driving for me as his Team boss.

Meanwhile, the rally car preparation side of the Dukeries Garage business was continuing to expand very rapidly, and as the reputation of the Ford Cortina GT and the Lotus Cortina began to spread, more and more of our better-off-customers were beginning to ask for them. This presented us with a slight problem. Because Mansfield is situated in what was then a fairly poor mining area, the local Ford dealers didn't tend to stock these models, simply because there wasn't that much call for them. People in that part of the world were generally only interested in the cheaper Anglias and 1200s. As a result, we were having great difficulty in getting hold of Cortinas to convert into rally cars.

Leafing through the trade magazines one day, Jim Adams then noticed that a company in London, called Clarke & Simpson, were offering Cortina GTs and Lotus Cortinas for immediate delivery. He got straight on the phone to them and arranged to buy the first of quite a few cars that we took from then, forging a connection that was soon to play a very significant part in my life. With a posh location in Sloane Square, from where they were more accustomed to selling top-of-the-range models to the well-heeled residents of Kensington, Chelsea and Knightsbridge, they were clearly intrigued by these two rather unlikely lads from 'up North' who kept coming down to raid their showroom.

It is extraordinary to recall that at that time the list price for a brand new Cortina GT was £707, while our set charge for preparing such a car for a major International event like the RAC Rally was exactly £100, including parts and labour. For that you'd get a sump shield, tank guard, a wood-rimmed steering wheel, wide rim wheels and maybe even a driver's seat. At today's prices, a fully prepared World Rally Car is likely to set you back at least £400,000 while even a more modest Group N production car works out at around £85,000. And, even so, there are still plenty of takers.

Once bitten by the rallying bug, you often find that it takes hold of you like a disease. I make no apologies for using the word 'disease' because, over the years, I have seen businesses, marriages and relationships infected and destroyed as addicts get hooked to the point where the sport takes priority over everything else in their lives.

In this respect, I'm afraid that I was no exception in my younger days and by the early part of 1966 my marriage to Jean was in serious trouble as a result. In a very literal sense our married life had got off to a bumpy start when, following the wedding in Nottingham Register Office in 1963 and the reception in a local pub, we set off to spend our honeymoon driving around the South Coast only to be rammed up the back by another car while stationary at some traffic lights in Salisbury. Poor Jean suffered a fairly serious whiplash injury and ended up spending the second night of her honeymoon in hospital.

Later, it was rally cars that were responsible for causing irreparable damage to our relationship. It got to the point where I was spending every available moment of my spare time either working on my car or driving it in events.

Weekend after weekend I would be out all night on the Saturday, taking part in a rally somewhere. I would arrive home at dawn and then snatch a couple of hours sleep before going back to work at 10.00am. By Sunday evening I would be totally knackered and would fall asleep in front of the television. There was one period, I remember, when I was away rallying seven weekends on the trot. Not surprisingly, Jean eventually decided that she was not prepared to put up with this sort of routine any more and went back to live with her parents.

Shortly after we had separated I happened to be talking to Clarke & Simpson about a particular car that Jim and I were trying to buy and in the middle of the call Robert Simpson himself came on the line. Being a rather traditional ex-military type there was no preamble, no 'David' or 'Mr Sutton'. Instead, he went straight to the point with a brusque: "Now then, Sutton, are you available to talk privately for a few minutes?" He went on to tell me that his Ford sales manager was leaving and that he was looking for a replacement. "I've heard from my staff that you're a bright lad and I wondered if you might be interested?" he added.

The timing couldn't have been better. I was ready to move on. Apart from that, it occurred to me that a fresh start and a complete change of scenery might help Jean and me to save our marriage. I agreed to go down to London for an interview at the end of which I was formally offered the job. I was also informed that Clarke & Simpson sales staff were paid a straight salary rather than on a commission basis and that I would be on £1,900-a-year. I nearly fell off my chair. I was 26 and I didn't think there was that much money in the whole world.

I went back home and rang Jean to tell her what was happening and to ask her whether she would like to come with me and see if we could make things work again. She agreed and a few weeks later, with a borrowed Transit van containing all our worldly possessions, an overdraft facility of £500 to tide us over the first few weeks and an ex-works Lotus Cortina, I set off in traditional Dick Whittington style to a new job and a new life in London.

SLOANE RANGER

I didn't exactly get off to a flying start in my new job. Jean and I couldn't afford to live in Central London so we moved into an apartment in Woking and for the first week or two I was late for work almost every morning as I struggled to find my way in through the rush hour traffic. Not even the smart new Cortina GT demonstrator that I had been given as an office car was much use in this respect, although I have to admit that it did help to ease the pain.

When I did eventually arrive, breathless and apologetic, and made my way to my desk on the mezzanine floor of the showroom, I found myself in an entirely alien environment at first. In the middle of the Swinging Sixties, London seemed a technicolour world away from the drab monochrome of Mansfield. And Sloane Square itself, being at the posh end of Chelsea's super-trendy Kings Road, was at the very epicentre of the exciting social revolution that was taking place.

Clarke & Simpson had only a small three-car showroom but it enjoyed a prime location just a few yards from the entrance to Sloane Square tube station, nestling between the Royal Court Theatre and the Royal Court Tavern. Tim Clarke and Robert Simpson had started the business shortly after the war, having first got to know each other in the Army, and had built it up into a successful multi-franchise dealership, selling Rileys, Wolseleys, Jaguars, Ramblers and top-of-the-range Fords to the well-heeled residents of what must then have been one of the wealthiest residential catchment areas in the country.

For a 26-year-old from what was still regarded as the frozen wastes of the North by anyone living South of Watford, the immediate culture shock was considerable and manifested itself in many different ways. For instance, having been brought up by my father to believe that you only ever wore a white shirt and a sober tie for business, I was quite shocked to find my fellow salesmen coming to work in pink shirts, green shirts, mauve shirts and even boldly striped shirts with contrasting white cuffs and collars. They seemed to have a different colour for each day of the week, often garishly teamed with a psychedelic tie. I remember thinking: "Hang on a moment! I'm not too sure about this."

The process of my settling in was not made any easier by the fact that Robert Simpson had hyped my arrival in advance, telling everybody that he had got this young chap coming down from Mansfield who was going to bring "a breath of fresh air" to the business. Needless to say, this served only to ensure that the rest of the sales team had already decided to hate my guts even before I'd set foot in the place.

Two people, in particular, came to my rescue in those early days. One was Tony Woolley, the sales manager in charge of the Jaguar division, who occupied the desk next to me on the mezzanine floor. Now, sadly, no longer with us, Tony, whose dress sense was especially stylish, took me under his wing and taught me everything I ever needed to know about the London motor trade.

Further very welcome moral support came from Robert Simpson's daughter, Jill, who worked in the Accounts Department. Back at Dukeries in Mansfield, when we first started buying Cortinas from Clarke & Simpson, Jim had gone down to London to collect one of the early cars and had returned with a big grin on his face, raving about the cracking blonde in Accounts. Later, when it was my turn to go down and pick up a car, I had kept my eyes peeled but had not spotted anybody who fitted that description. Now, at last, I could see exactly what Jim had been getting so excited about!

Both Jill and I were married at that time so there was no question of our relationship going beyond a casual friendship. Basically, Jill just felt sorry for me because she could sense that

I was struggling to find my feet. She kept me posted about everything that was going on, let me know what was being said about me behind my back and generally did her best to help me get to know the ropes.

After three weeks I still hadn't managed to shift a single car and spent most of my time sitting at my desk, gazing anxiously into space as I waited for the phone to ring with an order and starting to worry that maybe I had made a big mistake. My first sale came as an enormous relief. It was to a lady doctor from Harley Street who, like most people at that time, picked up on my accent and asked where I came from. I had started to use the novelty value of what was then still quite a strong East Midlands nasal twang to my own advantage, amused to discover how many of our posh clients had vague up-country connections coupled with some rather quaint notions about the geography of the UK north of Swiss Cottage.

"I say, I was shooting up in the Dales last weekend – is that anywhere near you? " was the kind of response I would get from people when I revealed that I hailed from Mansfield. Or: "I've got an aunt who lives in Harrogate – is that in your neck of the woods?" I soon realised that it was actually quite a good way of breaking the ice so I quickly abandoned any attempt to tone the accent down and, if anything, actually ratcheted it up a notch or two.

It wasn't only the toffs who were drawn to Clarke & Simpon's Chelsea showroom. At the height of the flower power era a couple of hippie types in psychedelic headbands wandered in one day to enquire about an E-type Jaguar. I didn't recognise them but noticed that one of the girls in the office was jumping up and down behind their backs in a high state of excitement, pointing and mouthing: "Do you know who that is!?" I made an excuse and left them to look over the car while I went to find out what all the fuss was about and was then breathlessly informed that they were two of Fleetwood Mac. That didn't mean a lot to me at the time (this was before they reached their peak) and I have to confess that I couldn't tell you exactly which two members of the group they were. But I recall that I did manage to sell them the Jag!

On another occasion I was instructed to take a Rambler demonstrator down to Virginia Water, where a wealthy client had expressed interest in buying one. The Rambler, a big right-hand drive American estate car for which Clarke & Simpson were the London distributors, had exactly the sort of rugged OTT look that would appeal to a rock star. I arrived at the house and was shown into a room where, sitting with some other young people in a circle on the floor was a bloke with green hair.

He didn't say much but simply got up, went outside and walked around the car a couple of times. He then thanked me politely, went back in and rejoined the circle without another word. I, meanwhile was shown into the kitchen and offered a cup of tea by a member of the staff who returned after a few minutes and announced: "Yes, he'll have that. Would you be interested in taking one of his other cars in part-exchange?" I was then shown a veritable fleet of vehicles from which I picked out a white Jaguar and the deal was done. Which is how it came about that I am able to claim Elton John among my more illustrious clients!

Gradually, I began to achieve some quite decent sales figures. More significantly, as far as the future was concerned, some of my loyal rally car customers from Mansfield followed me to London. As a result, I was able to persuade Clarke & Simpson after a few months that it would be worthwhile to open a specialist Competitions Department. What this meant in practice was that I was allocated a corner of the workshop and allowed to use one of the mechanics to help me prepare the occasional rally car for clients.

At the same time, I was also given leave to take my own Lotus Cortina into the workshop in the evenings to work on it after hours. My off-duty rallying activities were still expanding quite fast at this time. As soon as I had arrived in London I had joined both the London Motor Club and the Sutton and Cheam Motor Club and I was managing to get involved in an event of some kind or other almost every weekend.

By 1967 I had driven all of the Home Internationals, including the famous Gulf London Rally, of which I have particularly fond memories – and not just because I got a kiss from Susan Hampshire as we were flagged away in Manchester! A special non-Championship event, the Gulf London was, for my money, one of the most fabulous rallies ever, even though it was also a real ball-breaker, involving five days and four nights of non-stop driving.

Like most rally enthusiasts of my vintage, I look back with a certain nostalgic longing to the days when all the main events were tests not just of sophisticated driving skills and the latest technological development but also of endurance, stamina and mechanical improvisation. As I delight in telling today's young drivers, they hardly know they're born! In my view, they have things far too cushy most of the time – only three days from start to finish, no night driving, a luxurious, fully-catered motor home to relax in between stages while an army of mechanics works on your car and a comfortable hotel bedroom to go to every evening.

In my driving days, before the demands of worldwide television coverage caused everything to change, events like the RAC Rally routinely required you and your co-driver to keep going virtually non-stop from the Saturday morning right through until the Monday night. And that was just the first leg! It was then back on the road on Tuesday morning right through until the finish on Wednesday evening.

Apart from the Monday night, the only sleep you got in the whole five days was limited to the catnaps you could snatch in the car at the roadside 'rest halts' at each time control. And the chances were that you would have to spend most of your time during those breaks working on the car with whatever mate was following you with a toolbox, a set of spare wheels and a few cans of petrol in the back of a battered estate car. Not even the factory teams had anything like the sort of set-up they have today. I remember it being a major talking point when Ford decided to start carrying their spares in a Transit van rather than a Granada Estate.

At the risk of sounding like a classic boring old fart, I have to say that the old-style rallies were much more demanding than most modern events and a greater all-round test of man, if not machine. At the same time, they were also a lot more fun in the days when the competition was perhaps not quite so cut-throat and there was room for a bit of relaxation before and afterwards.

One of the toughest events in Europe at the time was the Circuit of Ireland, which involved 1000 miles of closed road special stages. It also included a two-night stopover in Killarney that always coincided with the end of Lent, when the streets of the town would be strewn with paralytic Irishmen and the bars would be full of stunning young colleens who would descend in droves from the surrounding mountains, looking for a good time and even, possibly, a husband. On one never-to-be-forgotten occasion, my co-driver, who had perhaps better remain nameless, fell so deeply in love with one of these green-eyed beauties that I had a terrible job getting him back into the car for the final day.

Although, by now, I was trying to concentrate on driving Internationals, I did return from time to time to do local events in the East Midlands and actually managed to win the East Midlands Championship one year with my dear friend, Mike Giles, as my co-driver. Despite such occasional triumphs, I never had any illusions about my limited talents as a driver and certainly never entertained any serious ambition of trying to break into the big league. I had come to accept, long before I finally retired altogether in the early 1970s, that whatever strengths I had lay in preparing cars for other people. At Clarke & Simpson, the Competitions Department was really starting to make a real name for itself and had been appointed by Ford as one of seventy selected RS dealers around the country who were officially franchised to sell and service their dedicated rally cars. That was certainly a feather in our caps at the time, although not quite such a unique honour as my boss at first imagined when he was presented with a tie emblazoned with the initials RS, which he took to stand for Robert Simpson!

A clear indication of how highly we were regarded by Boreham came when wealthy Nottinghamshire farmer and rally enthusiast Toby Sheppard, a very close friend as well as one of my best clients, decided that he wanted to drive the 1967 Tulip Rally in Holland and asked me to prepare a car for him.

Ford were about to unveil the Mk II Lotus Cortina and I managed to talk them into letting me have one several weeks ahead of the official launch date so that I could get it ready in time for Toby to be able to use it in the Tulip. Clarke & Simpson thus had the honour of being responsible for the Mk II's debut appearance in a major International rally.

While this brought us plenty of kudos, it was as nothing compared to the totally unexpected coup I managed to pull off the following year. In 1968 the first-ever London-Sydney marathon was uppermost in everybody's minds, occupying most of the manufacturers' time, not to mention a large chunk of their annual budgets. My own involvement was to prepare a Lotus Cortina for an Indian gynaecologist, who subsequently got as far as Bombay before vanishing completely, never to be seen or heard of again. I often wonder what became of him and his car, but as we'd been paid in advance I didn't lose too much sleep over it.

Meanwhile, during the lead-up to the event, I had received a call one day from John Davenport, then a well-known motorsport journalist as well as a respected Works co-driver, who asked me if it would be convenient for him to pop round and introduce me to a couple of friends of his who were interested in what we were doing at Clarke & Simpson. He then amazed me by turning up at the showroom accompanied by two

Finnish gentlemen whom I recognised instantly as Timo Mäkinen and Hannu Mikkola. Few would argue that Timo was by far and away the fastest and most famous driver in the world at that time while Hannu was already a rising star, so I was enormously flattered when they invited me to join them for lunch.

The main talking point, of course, was the London-Sydney and it emerged that although BMC were heavily involved, Timo, for reasons that were never fully explained to me, had declined to take part in the event. I jokingly suggested that maybe he would like to drive my newly arrived Escort Twin Cam in the RAC instead. He laughed politely at this suggestion and the conversation then moved on to other matters.

Later in the afternoon, however, the receptionist buzzed through to tell me that a foreign-sounding gentleman, with a name she hadn't quite been able to catch, was on the line from a public call box at Heathrow and wanted to speak to me urgently. It was Timo and I could hardly believe my ears when I heard him say in his broken English that he had considered my offer and that if I were serious he would be delighted to take me up on it.

At this point panic immediately started to set in. Why had I ever opened my big mouth? How could a little outfit like ours possibly begin to think about getting involved at this sort of level? Where was the money going to come from? How could I provide service? Who was going to supply the engine and tyres? Could I find a sponsor? What would my boss say? Surely I would get fired? Even as these thoughts were racing through my mind I was aware of a voice that I vaguely recognised as my own confirming enthusiastically that of course I was serious and that, yes, no problem, I would start getting things organised straightaway.

This story provides a pretty good example of my impulsively positive approach to any really good opportunity that arises, which is, quite simply, to say yes first and then worry about how to do it afterwards. I'm a great believer in the idea of nothing ventured, nothing gained.

The boss, when I explained the situation, said it was fine by him as long as I could put some kind of deal together, making it clear that this was my responsibility. My next call was to my good friend Toby Sheppard, whose immediate reaction was that if the World No 1 were going to be driving, then he would be more than happy to put up some of the money. At this point I decided that I would go direct to Ford to see if I could get any help from them.

I rang Henry Taylor, then Competitions Manager at Boreham, and told him: "Henry, I've got a very interesting piece of news for you, but it is something I can only really discuss with you eyeball-to-eyeball." Sensing that it was something important he agreed without hesitation to see me first thing the next morning.

"So, what can I do for you, David?" he asked casually as I breezed into his office at nine o'clock sharp. When I then revealed that I had persuaded Timo Mäkinen to do the RAC in a Ford Escort he nearly fell off his chair. "Are you sure?" he queried excitedly. "I am," I replied. "And I think we have a good chance of winning."

The purpose of my visit, I added, was to see if he might be able to help us by putting in a word in for us with Goodyear, whose tyres Ford were using. And to ascertain whether there was any possibility that he might be able to lend us a factory engine and perhaps a few spares?

This was the first of several occasions during my career when I was politely invited to step outside a senior motor industry executive's office and wait in the corridor while he and his fellow managers considered my case. After a few minutes I was called back in. "Look, David," said Henry. "We've had a think about this and rather than mess about lending you bits and pieces, why don't we just lend you a complete car?"

Now it was my turn to register amazement. To be given the opportunity to work on a Factory Escort – the one I was given was an ex-1000 Lakes Twin Cam that had been driven by Ove

Andersson – was not something I had envisaged. It then turned out that because Ford were concentrating so much time, effort and money on the London-Sydney, they had not bothered with an entry in the RAC, so they could hardly believe their luck when I suddenly walked through the door offering them the chance to be represented with the World No 1 in the driver's seat.

I was really confident now that we would win the event, maybe a little too confident. It was this that led me to make what I afterwards recognised, with the wisdom of hindsight, to have been a massively wrong decision. Because Ford had loaned us their car, this left my own car free, so I thought I might as well go ahead and drive in the rally myself, leaving the running of Timo's car to my mechanics and the team of friends and helpers that I had assembled to man the support vehicles. These volunteers included Jim Adams and several other colleagues from the Dukeries days, all of them thrilled to be involved.

Timo led the rally convincingly for the first three days and then had what should have been a minor problem with a loose water hose clip. Impatient, as ever, to get on and not waste a moment, he insisted on a quick repair rather than full replacement with the result that the clip worked loose again a bit further down the road, leading to the head gasket failure that put him out of the event. I have been haunted for the last thirty-five years by the thought that if only I had been at that service point, instead of out driving the rally, I might have managed to get the fault sorted out properly there and then, in which case we would almost certainly have gone on to an historic victory. One thing is for sure – there was nothing faster through the forests that weekend than Timo Mäkinen in our car.

The event was finally won by Simo Lampinen and John Davenport, with me a distant but respectable 12th overall. One nice memory is that the first person to shake my hand when I arrived on the finishing ramp was Timo himself. And at least I could console myself with the thought that we had taken an important step forward insofar as we had proved that at Clarke & Simpson we could build cars that were capable of winning International events when driven by the world's top drivers. Some months later I got a chance to work with Timo again when Ford asked us to repeat the exercise by entering him for what was to be his one and only appearance in the Circuit of Ireland. Here, again, he was leading at the point when he was forced to retire, this time by a broken differential.

An interesting little footnote to that earlier RAC Rally episode is that, despite having the services of the World No 1, it was the only time in my experience when the a co-driver was paid more than the driver. Because he had made the initial approach to us, rather than the other way round, Timo had agreed to drive the event for a much reduced fee of just £50 plus expenses while Paul Easter, his regular and well-renowned co-driver throughout his BMC days with the Mini Cooper, insisted on £100, still a small fortune in 1968.

Our sales of the Escort were increasing rapidly by now and, as the successor to the Mk II Lotus Cortina began to establish its reputation as *the* great rally car of all time, we found that we simply couldn't get hold of enough cars to satisfy the demand. Eventually, I took the unprecedented step of writing to Walter Hayes, the supremo in charge of all Ford Motorsport, to explain the problem and to ask if there was any way he could help out. To my surprise and delight, he promptly ordered the factory to produce twelve extra cars for special delivery to Clarke & Simpson.

Meanwhile, the management of the Ford Competitions Department at Boreham had changed and was now under the direction of the legendary Stuart Turner. When our telephone receptionist called through to announce that the great man himself was on the phone, demanding to speak to me personally, my immediate thought was that it was one of my friends playing a joke. I was then even more surprised to hear him asking whether he could make an appointment to come and see me in

Sloane Square. This was most definitely a case of the mountain coming to Mohammed!

When he duly arrived at the Sloane Square showroom I soon realised that the real underlying purpose of his visit was to check out our workshop. Clearly satisfied with the set-up we were able to show him, he went on to explain that Boreham was struggling to build enough cars for its own competition programme while also meeting demand from Ford dealers around the world and that it had therefore been decided to appoint two or three sub-contractors to build replica Works cars. We had been selected, along with British Vita Racing and Roger Clark Cars, to build a number of replica Escorts, starting, in our case, with a Twin Cam for Ford Norway that was to be driven by the extremely talented Trond Schea.

Our orders from Stuart were very clear and very precise. We were to put every bolt, every washer and every clip exactly where we were told to put them. We were not to introduce even the slightest variation. At the same time, there seemed to be absolutely no reason why we could not build replica cars for our own customers as well as for Boreham and for other Ford companies.

We were soon preparing the best Ford Escorts in Europe, greatly assisted by Boreham, who were keeping us constantly up to date with all the latest specifications. The only restriction was the understanding that we would keep our private customer cars six months behind the Boreham cars in terms of development, to allow time for any experimental new components to be fully approved.

The year 1970 was almost a repeat of 1968, with manufacturers once again concentrating on a major new marathon event, this time the 16,000-mile World Cup London-Mexico Rally. Stuart Turner, in his infinite wisdom, decided to enter seven cars, four to be built at Boreham and the other three by the sub-contractors.

My brief was to prepare a car for yet another of the Flying

Finns, Rauno Aaltonen. Known as 'The Professor' because of his rather earnest academic approach and his insistence on knowing everything there was to know about the technical specification of the cars he drove, Rauno eventually finished an impressive 3rd overall behind Hannu Mikkola, who was in one of the Factory cars, and second best of the seven Escorts. In an event of this calibre, this was an exceptionally good result for a private Team. And we would have done even better had it not been for a problem with the car that could have been avoided if only certain information about the need for modifications to a particular component had been passed on to us by Ford.

I need hardly remind anyone that the rally scene in this country in the early seventies was totally dominated by Roger Clark, the only home grown talent at the time who could give the Scandinavians a run for their money. I did, however, manage to find a couple of other Brits who could get close to him on a good day, namely Mike Hibbert and Barry Lee. Both these two, at various times, drove our Clarke & Simpson Escort, with its famous registration CS1. This, incidentally, was later sold by Robert Simpson for just £800. Today that number would probably be worth one hundred times that amount.

Mike Hibbert joined the Clarke & Simpson sales team shortly after winning the Scottish Championship in 1969 and although he would be the first to admit that he was a pretty hopeless salesman – as the nephew of the Earl of Inchcape I think he was probably just a bit too gentlemanly for that line of work! – he was a very good and a very fast driver. Also, I have to say, a very cheap driver, insofar as he never so much as put a dent in any of our cars despite being blindingly quick and doing very well for us.

Mike was still only in his twenties when he decided to retire prematurely in 1973, after the fuel crisis had caused the cancellation of the Scottish Rally in which he was to have made his full Works debut with Ford. He went on to launch his own very successful petrol station business in Scotland but, in some ways, it was a pity that he never fulfilled his potential as one of the best young amateur drivers around in that era. We remained close friends and I was delighted to be able to entice him out of retirement many years later to drive for me in some Historic events.

Barry Lee was someone else who, in my opinion, could have gone on to greater things if he had stuck to rallying instead of switching his attention to hot rod racing. I remember building him a brand new car for the Welsh Rally at a time when he had not driven in any kind of event for over a year and on the first special stage he slotted into second place behind Roger Clark and stayed there throughout. Later, he drove the RAC for me in the days when it was virtually impossible for any British driver apart from Roger to finish in the Top Ten and was lying 6th when a monumental accident in Dodd Forest in the Lake District left the car badly out of shape and destroyed his chances of a very good result. I always felt that if he had concentrated on his rallying and had developed his skills, he had the potential to be up there with the best of them. But Barry was a flamboyant character who preferred to be a large fish in a small pool, which was why he turned to hot rod racing instead.

Meanwhile, another bright new talent had emerged unexpectedly much closer to home. Jill Robinson, the boss's daughter, had begun to take an interest in rallying from the moment I arrived in Sloane Square with my Lotus Cortina and opened the Competitions Department. Later, she came along with her husband, Peter, and their son Guy, to watch me taking part in a rally and remarked afterwards that she wouldn't mind having a go herself one day. My immediate and disgracefully chauvinistic reaction was: "You can't possibly drive a rally car – you're a woman!" But, as I was to discover, this was factually as well as politically incorrect.

Jill kept on badgering me about it until, in 1969, I eventually gave in and got hold of a wrecked Lotus Cortina from Boreham that we completely rebuilt for her with a new body shell. After a few dummy runs, I then entered her in a club rally in the Forest of Dean, with Stuart Johnson as her co-driver, convinced that her first taste of the real thing would put her off for life,instead of which she actually did rather well, jumping out of the car at the finish with a look of pure exhilaration on her face to announce excitedly: "That was fantastic! When are we going to do the next one?"

From that moment on there was no stopping her and during the ensuing ten years she went on to establish herself as one of the world's top women rally drivers, winning the British Ladies title no less than three times in the early seventies. There was no denying that she was blessed with more natural talent than I ever had and in the end I retired from driving completely to concentrate on helping to run her career.

By that time, in 1974, we were married. Our first marriages had both ended some time before our relationship progressed beyond mere friendship. As far as Jean and I were concerned, our attempt at reconciliation had failed purely because of my continuing obsession with rallying. If anything, this had taken an even stronger hold on me following the move to London and I couldn't in any way blame Jean for once again walking out on me. Selfishly, I had made no real effort to change my ways.

In the meantime, Jill's marriage to Peter had also collapsed for reasons that had nothing to do with me. Inevitably, in the aftermath, we tended to cry on each other's shoulders but even then it was quite a while before we realised that we had more in common than a shared passion for rallying.

It was one drink too many that finally and rather fortuitously threw us together. I was coming back from a party in the West End when I was randomly breath-tested and found to be just one milligram over the 80-milligram limit, a fractional amount but enough to cost me my licence. Unable to drive, I was worried at first that I might lose my job but was then assured that there would be no problem as long the ban didn't affect my work in any way.

The rest of the sales staff helped me out with the demonstrations while others in the office gave me lifts whenever necessary. And as Jill and I were living not far from each other – she in Kingston and me in Teddington – it was only natural that she should offer me lifts to and from Sloane Square. This arrangement worked out particularly well since I was by now spending an increasing amount of time in the evenings personally preparing her rally car in the workshop after it had closed for the day and everybody else had gone home. Inevitably, in these circumstances, one thing soon led to another.

We were married at Caxton Hall in the summer of 1974 and our honeymoon was spent driving the 1000 Lakes Rally in Finland – in separate cars! In fact, we were late checking in at Heathrow for our flight to Helsinki, having come straight from a rather boozy wedding lunch at a hotel near the airport with Best Man Ivor Gordon and his wife Primrose, who had acted as our witnesses, and it was very much touch and go as to whether they would let us through to get on the plane. Jill saved the day by bursting into tears as she pleaded on our behalf and explained that we were flying off on our honeymoon, a bravura performance that so touched the hearts of the check-in staff that arrangements were immediately made to drive us out to the plane as it waited on the tarmac!

Jill's son Guy, then 14, had predictably sacrificed the pleasure of attending the wedding in favour of going out to Helsinki in advance with the mechanics. It had been agreed that I would drive Jill's Escort while she borrowed Pentti Airikkala's Alfa Romeo and I would be lying if I denied that there was a certain amount of needle between the newly-weds. Natural modesty prevents me from saying which of us eventually prevailed in this early marital confrontation.

GOING IT ALONE

Jill was soon to become, quite literally, the 'Golden Girl' of British rallying. Her arrival on the scene coincided with the beginnings of major commercial sponsorship in rallying and I think it is probably true to say that I negotiated the first-ever four-figure deal in rallying when Benson & Hedges agreed to sponsor her famous gold Escort.

Up until this time it was really only the tyre and oil companies who had stickers on the cars and, in many cases, all they would give you in return for that was free or discounted product. The most you could ever expect by way of cash sponsorship was £25-per-rally or maybe, in exceptional cases, £100-a-year. That all started to change when the tobacco companies, in particular, spotted the powerful potential that motorsport offered for brand placement.

Benson & Hedges were one of the first to get involved and were particularly interested in Jill because their brand was targeted primarily at women. They then had the bright idea of painting the car in exactly the same shade of gold as their distinctive pack and although this cost a fortune it was so effective that when we did a formal presentation outside their head office in the City, it stopped the traffic. I remember one of their senior managers making a point of taking a pack of cigarettes from his pocket and tossing it onto the bonnet. The colour match was so perfect that the pack seemed to disappear.

The car made its debut in this striking new livery in the RAC Rally, where it achieved maximum impact thanks to a couple of happy coincidences. That year, for the only time in the history of the RAC, the organisers decided to run all the lady drivers at the front and as Jill had drawn No 1 she was first off the ramp,

43

in front of all the cameras.

I found myself standing next to a Benson & Hedges promotions executive who was getting so carried away with it all that I thought I had better sound a word of caution, warning him that rallying was a high risk sport where anything could happen and that there were was no guarantee that we wouldn't be left with egg on our faces by the end of the day. But as he watched Jill drive off amid a barrage of photographers' flash bulbs, he turned to me with a huge smile on his face and said: "David, we've had our money's worth already."

It was probably just as well that he thought that way because four stages later the engine blew up and we had to retire. Despite this disappointment, the company decided to sponsor Jill for the whole of the next year's British Championship and that was when I negotiated the £1,000 deal, an unheard of amount in those days. Sadly, it turned out to be a totally disastrous campaign during which the car failed in every single event for one reason or another and the following year Benson & Hedges pulled out and decided to spend their budget on one-day cricket instead!

It wasn't that they felt we had let them down in any way. What they had discovered, of course, was that with cricket you could stick your visiting corporate VIPs in a comfortable box in the stand, the wives could wear their best frocks and everybody could sit down to eat smoked salmon sandwiches and strawberries and cream, washed down with champagne, while they watched the action. One of the great problems with rallying, as far as this sort of sponsorship is concerned, is that it provides little or no opportunity to entertain a static crowd. Corporate bosses tend to be very much influenced by their wives in these matters – and what fashion-conscious female wants to be dragged off into the forest in green wellies and a Barbour, only to be covered in mud and caught in a hail of flying gravel!?

At the same time, however, there were plenty of other people around who were warming to exactly this sort of excitement and the sport was continuing to attract more and more fans and an increasing amount of media attention. As a result, we found ourselves getting involved from time to time in the odd publicity stunt.

In particular, we had great fun preparing an Escort for the RAC Rally that was to be driven by Jill with veteran disc jockey Jimmy Savile, now Sir Jimmy, as her co-driver. This was part of an on-going campaign by the RAC at that time to update the old-fashioned image of rallying as the sort of pastime exclusively reserved for gentlemanly types in tweeds, flying helmets and goggles. The idea was to involve all sorts of top sports and showbiz stars in the hope of correcting this public perception, although the choice of the eccentric Sir Jimmy might possibly have been seen as taking things a little too far in the other direction.

At every time control on the first day thousands of people pressed forward to get a glimpse of the madcap DJ, then at the peak of his popularity. While Jill drove the stages, Jimmy, resplendent in outrageous orange overalls – and grumbling all the while about not being allowed to puff away on one of his trademark cigars while in the car! – contented himself with waving wildly to the fans, causing such a commotion that I suspect the organisers were actually quite relieved when we were once again forced to retire with engine failure.

Elsewhere, on a more serious level, the Competitions Department at Clarke & Simpson was enjoying great success and continuing to expand, with the recruitment of specialist mechanics such as Bob Marris, who went on to make a great name for himself at Boreham, and Ron Lumley, who was to stay with me for many years.

Another of the highlights of this period came following a visit to the 1000 Lakes Rally in Finland during which I was approached by a tall, skinny Finnish driver who asked me if I had a car available for the RAC Rally. It just so happened that I had a surplus of ex-Works Escorts at the time, having recently purchased the entire Harpers Team from Hong Kong.

The driver's name was Markku Alen. Still virtually unknown at that time, he had never driven outside Finland and because of this I decided that he should first do a smaller event in the UK in order to familiarise himself with the British forests. I therefore entered him in the Lindisfarne Rally and brought in the late, great Henry Liddon as his co-driver. Although they didn't feature in the results, owing to a broken suspension arm, Markku's special stage times were such a sensation that I hadn't been in the office more than ten minutes on the Monday morning after the event before Ford were on the 'phone. "Who's this new bloke you've got?" they wanted to know. "We've just had Liddon on saying he's the quickest thing that ever drew breath. Can you run him in the RAC if we loan you a car?"

At that time Markku knew only five words of English – "left", "right" and "vodka and tonic". To act as interpreter, he had brought his friend Ilkka Kivimaki over from Finland and it was Ilkka who took over as his co-driver for the RAC, a position he has held from that day to this. It was Markku's first RAC and only his second rally anywhere outside Finland and yet, quite amazingly, he managed to finish 3rd and would probably have won it quite convincingly had it not been for a minor incident on the very first day.

Frustratingly, this occurred during one of the 'Mickey Mouse' special stages that were always used as a curtain raiser for the RAC in those days. Usually held in and around the grounds of a stately home – Sutton Park in this instance – they were included largely for the benefit of the media and were disliked by all the drivers and team managers, who regarded them as an unnecessary gimmick, often turned into a complete lottery by the highly unpredictable nature of courses that were quite likely to include wet tarmac, dry tarmac, mud, grass, fallen leaves and just about every other surface you could imagine, making tyre selection almost impossible.

Markku had the misfortune to slide just slightly wide on some leaves and mud and crashed off the road, damaging the suspension and losing a huge amount of time as he struggled to get the car back on track. Had it not been for that one slip, his RAC debut would have been even more sensational. As it was, he still produced one of the most brilliant drives ever seen to haul himself back up to third place. And he went on from there to establish himself as one of the undisputed all-time greats of rallying during the course of an extraordinary 18-year partnership with Fiat/Lancia, leaving me to look back with the satisfaction of knowing that I had helped to launch his brilliant career.

My own career was also going pretty well at this time. I had risen from rookie salesman to Managing Director of Clarke & Simpson in less than seven years and would have had every reason to feel very pleased with life had it not been for the general economic gloom that had descended on the country as a whole. Although the Competitions Department was going well, the rest of the business was starting to suffer badly from the effects of the deep recession that had set in following the infamous winter of discontent in 1973/4.

The lights were literally going out all over the UK as the three-day working week was introduced in a desperate attempt to conserve energy in the wake of the OPEC oil price hike and our mechanics had to resort to building cars with miners' lamps strapped to their foreheads. At the same time, our regular car sales had slumped dramatically. Jaguars, for which there had previously been a waiting list of up to twelve months, were being offered for immediate delivery, but there were fewer and fewer takers and the cancellations were arriving daily.

By 1975, Robert Simpson had had enough. On the Thursday before Easter that year he called the entire workforce together and made the shock announcement that the company would be closing down that night and that, regrettably, nobody would be required to return to work the following week. Everybody would have to be paid off.

Along with mechanic Ron Lumley and one or two others, I stayed on for a few weeks just to tidy up and sell off the remaining stock, which included a number of rally cars in various stages of preparation. The realisation that the famous Clarke & Simpson Escorts had now gone forever was the saddest thing for me.

Robert Simpson had decided to move to Dorset and he was quite keen for Jill and I to go with him and start some sort of business down there together. But, at 35, I didn't think I was quite ready for Dorset. Instead, I decided to use my severance pay and the little bit of money that Jill and I had got saved up to launch my own specialist motorsport company, basically carrying on where the Competitions Department at Clarke & Simpson had left off. I was delighted when Ron Lumley agreed to come in with me on the new venture and it wasn't long before David Sutton (Cars) Ltd was officially in business. All we needed were some decent premises.

That problem was solved when, quite by chance, I bumped into Rod Cooper, a well-known driver at the time who also owned a tuning company in West London called Supersport Ltd. During the casual conversation that followed it emerged, rather fortuitously, that while I had got plenty of work on offer but nowhere to carry it out, he was in exactly the opposite situation, having a very well equipped workshop but very little work to put through it.

We soon did a deal whereby I agreed to rent space in his premises in Acton and, within weeks of moving in, Ron and I were not only keeping ourselves very busy, but were also providing employment for most of the Supersport mechanics as well. After four months, seeing the way things were going, Rod suggested that I might like to buy Supersport from him and take over the whole business, lock, stock and barrel. This I was able to do with the help of some financial backing from the late Jim Dewar, a wealthy accountant and rallying enthusiast whom I first got to know as a client at Clarke & Simpson and who went on to become a good friend.

Among the more valuable assets that came with the company was mechanic John O'Connor. John has been with me ever since, getting on for 30 years in all, and in that time we have been through thick and thin together. As far as I am concerned, there has never been a better or more experienced rally mechanic, a man of very few words but unlimited skills whose many claims to fame include a record fourteen-minute emergency gearbox change on an Audi, a feat that was preserved for posterity on a detailed minute-by-minute video, shot by a camera team who happened to be on the spot at the time. Some of John's other even more colourful exploits will be covered in later chapters.

In the very early days, David Sutton Cars survived mostly on re-building and preparing cars for Spanish customers, while also running a programme of events for Jill. Then, in 1976, I formed Team Avon Tyres with an amiable young Finn called Pentti Airikkala as the driver and John Davenport as co-driver. As it happens, their victory in the Snowman Rally proved to be John's swansong because shortly after that he was offered a top job with the RAC Motor Sports Division that left him no time for active rallying.

Pentti, meanwhile, quickly established himself as a force to be reckoned with, putting down an early and impressive marker when, in that year's 1000 Lakes Rally, he finished just fifty-one seconds behind winner Markku Alen in a Works Fiat. During the event I was introduced to Michael Kranefuss, then Head of Motorsport for Ford Europe, who seemed to spend most of the weekend shaking his head in apparent disbelief at what he was witnessing.

I later found out that he was making his first-ever visit to a World Rally Championship, but it wasn't just this that was the cause of his rather pained expression. What he couldn't quite understand was how a small team like ours, which consisted of no more than the rally car itself, a Granada Estate, two mechanics and me, was managing to beat the might of the full Ford Works team. Our achievement was made even more remarkable by the fact that their driver, the great Timo Mäkinen, had the advantage of being able to choose between two alternative types of tyres and wheel sizes while we were running on Avon tyres that cost just £8 each. And yet still we were managing to pull away.

Pentti went on to re-affirm his talent in the RAC, leading the event for the first three days, albeit with the possibility of disqualification for an alleged timing infringement hanging over him. I have always been confident that, had it been necessary for us to challenge the validity of the infringement, our appeal would have been upheld. But as things turned out, it never came to that. We lost the event because of a bad management decision on my part.

Towards the end of the rally Pentti started experiencing clutch problems. There was only one place in the entire last section where the clutch could have been changed and, unfortunately, I was not present at that particular service point because my own management car had broken down and I was left stranded some way behind the front-runners while I waited for it to be repaired. In my absence, the mechanics on the spot adjusted the clutch and Pentti – impatient, as ever, to get on – announced that it felt much better.

Two or three stages later, however, it expired altogether, allowing Roger Clark to cruise to an easy victory. I maintain to this day that if only I had been there at the service point, as I normally would have been, I would have insisted on a clutch change and Pentti would have won.

Incidentally, his co-driver on that occasion was Mike Greasley, a journalist at the time, now a motorsport management entrepreneur, who married my then secretary, Susan Deyes, a few years later.

While Pentti was burning it up in the British forests, yet another blindingly quick Finnish driver had burst upon the scene. Ari Vatanen first made his mark as a private driver in an old Opel and was immediately snapped up by Ford, who, at the end of 1976, offered me my first real Works contract to run him in the British Championship the following year, Pentti having been grabbed by Vauxhall. I wasn't quite sure whether to feel flattered or petrified. For a small team like ours to be given this high-flying, super-quick driver was both a great opportunity and a huge responsibility.

Any apprehension I might have felt was instantly dispelled when, in the very first event we did with him, he gave us our maiden International victory with a blistering win in the Mintex Rally in Yorkshire. We went on to win the Scottish Rally as well, which gave me particular pleasure since this has always been one of favourite events, partly because it was where I myself made my International debut as a driver.

In that same 1977 season Ari also drove eight World Championship events for Boreham but managed only one result with them and I think he rather enjoyed returning to his little team in West London, where he was having more success. Little did I ever imagine at that stage that, before too long, I would have the ultimate honour of making him World Rally Champion.

Peter Ashcroft, who was now in charge at Boreham, was a past master at gathering sponsorships from various companies and organisations, putting programmes together with particular drivers and then allocating them to outside teams, with various levels of support in terms of vehicles, engines, bodyshells and so on.

Ari's car had been sponsored by Gandy Brakes and the following year, in recognition of our successful campaign with him, we were delighted to be handed the Eaton Yale programme, with Hannu Mikkola as our driver. This was both an honour and a special pleasure for me because, ever since his surprise appearance at Clarke & Simpson with Timo Mäkinen ten years before, Hannu and I had kept in regular touch and I had become as close as anyone ever got to this very private man.

By this time, he was already well on his way to establishing his reputation as possibly the greatest driver of them all. That is certainly my own view, although, as a family friend and godfather to his eldest son, Juha, I am obviously biased. Nevertheless, I suspect that there aren't too many who would argue with that judgement. From the moment in Kenya in 1972 when I had watched from close quarters as he became the first European ever to win the Safari Rally, I had been totally in awe of his talents. To be given the chance to work with him was therefore an enormous bonus as far as I was concerned.

We enjoyed considerable success during that 1978 season, but our greatest and most satisfying victory came right at the end of the year, when the Ford strike meant that there could be no Factory involvement in the RAC Rally. As a result, the building of rally cars was sub-contracted to several outside teams and we were thrilled to be given the job of looking after both Hannu and Ari.

Ari's co-driver, Peter Bryant, made a mistake at a time control on the first day and they were subsequently disqualified, but Hannu went on to win in style, giving us our first-ever RAC Rally victory exactly ten years after we had led the event so convincingly with Timo, only to be cruelly disappointed at the last moment on that occasion.

Meanwhile, Ari's bad luck in the World Championship that year continued, with only one decent result out of four events. That characteristic all-or-nothing style for which he became notorious was already very much in evidence. With Ari it was usually a case of 1st, 2nd – or new body shell! There was nothing much in between. I clearly remember sitting with him one day in the little Italian restaurant that we used to frequent in West London, trying to raise his spirits after yet another disaster.

"What am I going to do?" he sighed, his head buried in his hands.

"Let's learn to finish rallies," I replied tersely.

He agreed, with a rueful smile, that this was obviously a sensible approach and we subsequently embarked together on a series of events that took us from Ireland to Madeira and quite a few places in between, producing several decent results.

Further afield, another highlight of that year came when we were asked to supply a car to America for the first time, Rod Millen and Mark Howard driving our Escort to victory in the North American Rally Cup. An incidental side effect of this venture was that Jill and I fell in love with California and decided to buy a little house in Newport Beach, just outside Los Angeles. We spent our summers there for the next ten years, flying out after the Scottish Rally in June and returning for the Manx Rally in September. Taking full advantage of Freddie Laker's revolutionary low-fare Skytrain, we could get two business class seats for the price of one.

It was in America that Jill was to drive her last competitive rally before retiring in 1980. She had started relatively late, at the age of 35, but enjoyed an extremely successful eleven-year career during which she drove in rallies all over the world. Apart from her three British Ladies Championship titles, the highlights included a 4th place finish in the Castrol Rally in South Africa and 18th overall in the RAC, when she was up against all the top male drivers of the day. I was always amused by the fact that although normally a very careful and mild-mannered driver, she was like a tigress once she got behind the wheel of a rally car.

Her decision to retire followed a rather nasty accident, after which she never fully regained her confidence. It happened on the test track at Bagshot, where she was trying out a car that we were preparing for a customer in Paraguay. The set-up at Bagshot featured an outer circuit with a rough, twisting 'snake course' running through the middle. Jill came bombing round the circuit and suddenly decided at the very last moment to dive off onto the snake course. Realising that she was going much too fast to take the turn, she then threw the car sideways to scrub off the speed but just caught the brick surround of a draining ditch with her back wheel and literally took off.

There was a golf course very close by and one of the things that stands out vividly in Jill's memory of the split second before she crashed to the ground is the vision, glimpsed out the corner of her eye, of an astonished golfer, frozen in mid-swing, his mouth hanging open in horror as he watched this car suddenly come flying through the trees next to the fairway.

First on the scene was the late, great Tony Pond. One of the top British drivers of the day, Tony happened to be there testing the latest Lancia for Fiat at the time, and, afterwards, Jill was quite flattered to think that such a big star had been sufficiently concerned about her to interrupt his programme and rush to her assistance, pulling her clear and draping his jacket over her. The car was a complete write-off and Jill herself was in a terrible mess. It was a hot day and she had been driving without a helmet and with the window partially open, both cardinal sins. As a result she suffered not only broken ribs, but also a severe gravel rash on her forearm that left scars she still bears to this day. In addition, there were also a lot of cuts and bruises to her face caused by branches and debris coming through the open window.

I got the sort of emergency call you always dread, summoning me to the hospital, and Jill insists that it remains the only time she has ever seen me looking really white with worry. Fortunately things weren't quite as bad as they appeared and Jill's main concern was for the car. Fortunately, we had a spare body shell and John O'Connor was able to rebuild it in time for the event. But although Jill got back behind the wheel as soon as possible she never quite recovered her nerve and decided shortly afterwards to call it a day, making her farewell appearance in Ohio in a Datsun loaned to her by Mark Howard.

It was on this occasion that she and Pauline Gullick became the first all-female crew ever to take part in a rally in the US. The Americans made a big fuss of them and were so concerned about their safety that they issued them with special flares to let off in the event of a break-down in the middle of nowhere, so that people could locate them quickly and go to the rescue. As it happens, Jill's only real worry was that there might be rattlesnakes about and she made it clear that if they did go off the road she would not be getting out of the car.

She hates snakes almost as much as I hate the dark!

The ladies were often treated in a rather patronising way in those days, both by male drivers and by event organisers, especially abroad. When Jill and Pauline made their debut in South Africa and finished in the top ten the organisers were caught so much by surprise that they had to send someone out in a hurry at the very last minute to find an extra trophy with which to present them.

Mind you, they were always a bit behind the times in South Africa. During that same event Jill was surprised to get an outraged call from the manager of her hotel, accusing her of having a man other than her husband in her room and ordering her to ensure that he left immediately. That man was me! Although we were indeed married by then, Jill had been booked in under her maiden name and when it came to the manager's notice that Jill Robinson was sharing a room with David Sutton he immediately suspected that she was flouting South Africa's strict moral conventions.

We, of course, were pure as the driven snow but others were not always so innocent and the sex police would have been hard put to keep up with all the hanky panky that is a regular and often rather entertaining feature of rallying's social scene. With the same group of people constantly being thrown together away from home in the same hotels around the world, there is plenty of opportunity to forge new and occasionally dangerous liasons. The late night traffic along upstairs corridors doesn't always stick to the correct lane and speculation at breakfast the next morning about who parked where is often rife.

Over the years I have watched all sorts of relationships develop and dissolve on the road, some of them in deliciously scandalous fashion. When word got around that I was writing this book I was amused to get calls, out of the blue, from several people anxious to know if they would be getting a dishonourable mention and, if so, whether they were likely to have some akward explaining to do when it came out! One mechanic drove halfway across the country and turned up on my doorstep to plead for discretion.

They can all relax - for the time being at least! This volume is aimed at the readers of Autosport and Motorsport News rather than the News of the World. I'll save the juicy bits for a rainy day when I might need to boost my pension fund.

Back in England in 1979, I had been surprised to get an invitation to lunch from Peter Ashcroft at Boreham. In rallying terms, this was as near to a Royal Command as you could get in those days and a definite indication that something pretty important was afoot. Even so, I was left speechless when Peter sat me down and announced that, following the 1979 RAC Rally, Ford would be pulling out of rallying altogether for a period of two years while they concentrated on developing a radically new car for the future and that he would like me to take over two of his drivers, complete with cars, sponsors and contracts, and run them in 1980 and 1981.

I was even more astonished when he added that my two drivers would be Hannu Mikkola and Ari Vatanen and that my objectives would be to win the British Championship in 1980 and the World Championship in 1981. What I was being offered was a unique opportunity but, even so, the decision to accept it was not quite as straightforward as it might have appeared.

For one thing, if we were to become, effectively, a full-time Works team, we would be left with little or no time to build and prepare cars for our other, private customers. However, it didn't take us too long to come to the conclusion that it had to be in the better long-term interests of the company to get involved in the sort of high-profile programmes that, at a stroke, would raise our status immeasurably. To be asked to do the World Championship on behalf of a major manufacturer and sponsor is the greatest honour you can aspire to in our business – apart from winning it, that is.

For a little fledgling company operating out of the back streets of West London to be launched into the world arena in this way, with all the people from Porsche and Peugeot and Fiat looking on, was an irresistible prospect. To be honest, I would probably have said yes to it even if it had meant chopping off both my arms! Meanwhile, I was still left facing the problem of where to get the money for the sort of equipment that these programmes would require. The answer here was provided by my old friend Toby Sheppard, who once again came up trumps with a major financial investment that was to extend for several years.

A few weeks later, with everything sorted out at my end, Peter Ashcroft and I arrived at the Aylesbury headquarters of sponsors Rothmans to get final approval for the arrangement and to hammer out all the finer points of the deal. It was here that I first met David Richards, who, as well as being Ari Vatanen's co-driver, was also the Rothmans motorsport consultant, a dual role that, although it didn't quite amount to a conflict of interest, did make my life as team manager a little awkward, putting our relationship under strain at one or two moments of high stress during the next two years.

At twenty-seven years of age, David was already showing signs of the ambition and entrepreneurial flair that have since helped him to become the undisputed World Rally supremo, second only to Bernie Ecclestone as a motorsport power broker. David it was who had introduced Rothmans to Ford in the first place and, right from the start, he proceeded to drive a hard bargain on their behalf, as anyone in his situation would have been expected to do. It was only after hours and hours of detailed discussions in Aylesbury that day that everybody eventually shook hands on the deal.

This allowed for twenty-two race entries in twelve events – five in the World Championship and five in the British Open Championship, plus two other events that had special local and national interest for Rothmans.

Ford contracted the drivers and co-drivers (Hannu was to be partnered, as usual, by the jovial Swede, Arne Hertz), paid their fees and then effectively loaned them back to David Sutton (Cars) Ltd.

Ford also supplied the drivers and co-drivers with contract cars – although I had to buy my own from my local Ford dealer! And, laughably by modern standards, we were given only two support vehicles – a Ford Transit van and a Granada Estate. I did feel that this was a bit on the tight side, but I wasn't about to make too much of a fuss. After all, here I was with the backing of two major sponsors in Rothmans and Eaton Yale, further support from Castrol and Dunlop and two of the greatest and fastest drivers of all time. As the head of a small company anxious to make a big name for itself, I had to admit that this amounted to the most incredible break.

I left the meeting a very happy man and went away to start preparing for what were to be two of the most extraordinary years of my life.

CHAMPIONS OF THE WORLD

Our campaign got away to a highly dramatic start as we experienced the extremes of total triumph and spectacular disaster within the first two events. We opened up with a resounding 1st and 2nd on the Mintex Rally, with the old maestro, Hannu Mikkola, showing his younger team mate how it should be done – although, to be fair, Ari had been briefed that his attack on the British Championship should be a steady point-scoring exercise rather than a death-or-glory bid for outright victories.

Following this impressive performance, we arrived in Portugal in confident mood for our next World Championship event, only to record a one-two of a rather different and less welcome nature. Towards the end of one of the special stages, we were running 4th and 5th, two minutes apart, when Hannu lost control on a corner and went off the road, the car plunging twenty or thirty yards down a steep, wooded slope before finally coming to rest on its roof.

The problem had been caused by worn tyres failing to grip at a point where, under a blanket of wet leaves, the surface changed suddenly from gravel to tarmac and Hannu knew instantly that Ari, following right behind him, was almost bound to fall into the same trap. Sure enough, exactly two minutes later, Ari and David careered off the road at precisely the same point, rolled down the slope and landed neatly on top of Hannu and Arne's car.

We had to wait until all the other eighty-odd cars had gone through before we were able to walk into the stage to assess the situation and there were a few anxious moments, listening to it all unfolding on the radio, before we were able to establish that the drivers were OK. The cars, needless to say, were complete write-offs and we actually had great difficulty in winching them up out of the ravine into which they had crashed. Although certainly unusual, such a double catastrophe has not remained unique in rally history. It was repeated almost exactly by Toyota on the Acropolis Rally in 1992 – and, by a further coincidence, Arne was one of the co-drivers on that occasion, too.

Putting this rather expensive and disappointing setback behind us, we re-entered the fray on the gruelling Circuit of Ireland, where Ari fought a close five-day battle with Jimmy McRae before narrowly losing out due to a minor indiscretion during the final night section. Hannu was not available for this event, due to the fact that he was driving for Mercedes on the Safari Rally, so his place in the Eaton Yale car was taken by the Irish rallying legend Billy Coleman who, unfortunately, was forced to retire through engine failure.

The next big International event on the schedule was the Acropolis, always one of my favourites, despite the fact that it is also one of the roughest, toughest, longest and hardest. Like the Circuit of Ireland – equally demanding in its own rather different sort of way, with all those twisting, bumpy, tarmac roads, where you can find yourself going through a dry stone wall before you know it – the Acropolis is famous for its great atmosphere. The setting is wonderful and the Greek people very welcoming.

I say this despite the fact that one of my mechanics ended up in a prison cell there one year. As far as the Team were concerned, that situation might have been a lot more serious were it not for the seventies fashion for bushy Afro hairstyles! Let me explain. Fuel rationing was in force in Greece at the time and the way the system worked was that you could only use your car on alternate weekends, depending on whether the registration number was odd or even.

Mechanics John O'Connor and David Ewles were caught out after they had been working overnight in the workshop. In the early hours of the morning, tired and anxious to snatch a few hours' sleep before getting back to work, they jumped into a vehicle that had been loaned to us by the local Ford importer and drove back to the hotel, forgetting that the car had a local number plate. Stopping on the way to fill up with petrol they were spotted by a lurking traffic cop, arrested and taken to the local police station where they were informed that the driver would have to be remanded in custody until his court appearance a few days later. It was actually John who had been driving, but realising that his presence on the rally as chief mechanic would be missed much more than David's would be, the pair of them did some quick thinking and decided to work a switch.

Looking at John now, such a model of greying, conservatively-coiffed respectability, it is hard to believe that he once sported an Afro fuzz of which even a member of The Jackson Five would have been proud - as did David Ewles. The two of them actually looked so similar that they had no problem fooling the policeman who had originally pulled them over and David it was who took the rap and was duly locked up. Not even the pleadings of the bigwigs from Ford could get him off, although we did manage to get his court appearance arranged to fit in as conveniently as possible with our rally schedule. He was eventually fined £50, while John found himself buying the drinks for the rest of the week!

Ford Greece was Ford Advanced Vehicle Operations' largest parts customer outside the UK so this was a very important market for them. At the same time, it was also a key territory for Rothmans, who held a substantial market share there. So, one way and another, there was increased pressure on us to do well.

I had gained some useful experience there a couple of years previously when I had entered a car for Billy Coleman. I had also spent quite a lot of time teaching the local Ford importer's mechanics how to prepare rally cars. Even so, I still find it almost impossible to believe that we managed to bring Ari Vatanen home as the winner with a team of just sixteen people. The following year we increased the head count to a massive twenty-one!

That's still nothing compared with today's major World Championship events, when Works teams such as Ford often assemble armies of mechanics and support crew numbering up to 100. But what we lacked in numbers we more than made up for with commitment and versatility. These days, a Factory team mechanic will often be allocated one corner of the car and that's all he ever gets to work on, week in, week out. If you're not careful, that can lead to boredom, apathy and a lack of team spirit. We have certainly never had the slightest problem in this respect and I believe that the way we operate brings the best out in people. We've also benefited over the years from a close, long-term relationship with people like Terry Hoyle, who supplied all our Rothmans engines, and Gartrac's David Bignold and Bill Payne, who have been supplying my body shells for thirty-five years.

We returned from Greece to record another double triumph, Ari celebrating the recent birth of his first child by storming to victory in the Welsh Rally, with Hannu in second place. This event has never been one of my favourites, despite the fact that my wife, Jill, won the Ladies Award there no less than eight times during her career. The trouble with it is that there's no great craic out there in the wilds, only the monotony of endless damp, slate-grey forest tracks.

I much prefer the Scottish Rally, if only because I have such fond, nostalgic memories of my own 1966 International debut there, plus four victories as a manager. Here, a few weeks after our clean sweep in the Welsh, we kept up our winning momentum with a repeat performance, the only difference being that Hannu reminded us all who was boss by pushing Ari back into second place.

From there we went on to the 1000 Lakes in Finland. I had always suspected that if only Ari could prove himself on this, his home event, then it might help to calm him down and to eradicate some of the driving errors that continued to spring largely from his impetuosity. In the end, we had to be content with a very good 2nd place, less than a minute behind Markku Alen – the second time that a team of mine had finished 2nd in the 1000 Lakes. But Ari did indeed show signs of just the sort of maturity that would be required of him if he were going to be a serious contender for the World Championship the following year.

Later in the summer Rothmans Spain invited us to take part in the CS Rally (formerly the Firestone Rally) where we were fairly soundly beaten into second place by Jorge Bagration in the mighty Rothmans-sponsored Lancia Stratos, a car that was later to end up in our Rally Car Museum in Daventry.

We then got back into winning form in the Cyprus Rally, but not with either of the regular drivers. Rothmans had been the sponsors of this event for many years so we obviously had to show the flag. Our problem was that it conflicted with practice for the San Remo, which was a higher priority for Ari and Hannu.

The Cyprus Rally is far from being one of the speedier events in the European Championship. Ari had won it in 1979, but did not make himself very popular when he remarked afterwards that a 30mph average on the stages was painfully slow. It is also blisteringly hot and uncomfortable and great care and concentration is therefore needed to secure a good result. Bearing all this in mind as I looked around for a likely stand-in driver, it seemed that there was only man for the job – the old fox, Roger Clark.

Roger and I quickly agreed terms and my choice was fully vindicated when he duly went on to win the event by a massive margin of eleven or twelve minutes. I look back on this with special satisfaction because it turned out to be Roger's last-ever International victory, a significant footnote in rally history with which I am very pleased and proud to be associated.

In San Remo, one of the most popular and enjoyable events on the World Championship rota, Hannu and Ari finished a respectable 2nd and 3rd and we moved on to the RAC with high expectations. It was now that I had the first of two major tactical rows with David Richards that basically arose out of the awkward situation in which he was wearing two hats, as both Ari's co-driver and the Rothmans motorsport consultant, and where my authority as Team Manager was always in slight danger of being undermined as a result.

It was when David discovered that the Team possessed only one special 5.3 crown wheel and pinion and that I had decided it should be given to Hannu Mikkola in the Eaton Yale car that we found ourselves on a collision course.

I felt that if anyone could be relied upon to get us a result then it had to be Hannu rather than Ari, but, quite understandably given his position, David questioned this. As it happened, my instincts proved right on this occasion when Ari proceeded to have a monumental crash and completely destroyed his car while Hannu finished a very good 2nd.

Because of the status of the RAC, Rothmans had insisted on running an extra car in the event and, once again, I found myself casting around for someone with the sort of experience and reliability that I was convinced would count for more than anything in terms of trying to guarantee a decent result. This time I went for Timo Mäkinen, the veteran three-times RAC winner, and once again it proved a shrewd choice. With the highly respected journalist and author Martin Holmes as his co-driver, Timo finished a very respectable 6th, despite suffering from a bad dose of 'flu.

My final score for the Rothmans Ford programme at the end of that first year was five outright victories plus seven second places. And with Ari winning the British Championship we had succeeded brilliantly in achieving the main target that had been set for us. Not at all bad for a small private Team! But that success had come at a price, as I was to discover almost before we'd stopped spraying the champagne around when my auditors revealed that David Sutton Cars had made a thumping great

With my mother, Dorothy, in the late sixties, presenting a picture of innocence as a choirboy in 1952 and with the rest of the family at my sister Lynda's 21st in 1971. (l to r) Jeffrey, me, Dorothy, Lynda, Philip and Stuart.

The Dukeries Garage (complete with des.res.above the showroom) where my career in Rallysport really began.

Stepping up at a Dukeries Motor Club prizegiving, with Jim Adams (far left) looking on, and - Tarantara! Tarantara! - heavily and thankfully disguised as I indulge an early passion for Gilbert & Sullivan.

Jim Adams with Mike Giles as co-driver on the Circuit of Ireland and (left) me with an early Cortina.

Toby Sheppard on the 1967 Tulip Rally (below) in the MK II Lotus Cortina that I persuaded Ford to let me have ahead of it's official launch.

Timo Makinen at Clarke & Simpson, taking delivery of a Twin Cam Escort for ice racing in Finland, in action in Ireland (below right) and on the 1968 RAC Rally (bottom).

Robert Simpson, Jill's father and my boss at Clarke & Simpson.

*The first ex-Works rally car
ever to be sold on by Ford. It
cost me just £400 and provided
me with my first drive in an
International Rally.*

*With co-driver Mike Giles after
winning the Bruce Robinson
Rally in 1968.*

Barry Lee in action (above) and Mike Hibbert relaxing (right), two of the very few Brits, apart from Roger Clark, who could give the Finns and Scandinavians a run for their money back in the Seventies.

Barry was in 6th place on the RAC when this happened.

Jill Robinson hangs on grimly as her new ex-Works Cortina makes its debut in 1968 with me at the wheel.

Jill and I on the Ypres Rally in 1977.

Ooops! Jill destroyed this brand new Escort while testing at Bagshot three days before it was due to be shipped to Paraguay. It was re-shelled and shipped within a week.

Rauno Aaltonen in action in South America during the 1970 London - Mexico and (below), Hannu Mikkola on his way to victory in FEV 1H in 1970 (right) and in the 1995 Anniversary event in H1 FEV.

financial loss of £100,000 on the year. Needless to say, that wiped the smile off my face pretty quickly.

I have to admit that I've never been the greatest businessman even at the best of times – especially at the best of times, you could say! The truth is that I had allowed myself to get so carried away with the need to make the most of the fantastic opportunity that had fallen into my lap that I had adopted a rather cavalier attitude towards the bottom line, not really caring whether we made a profit or a loss as long as I could be there with my Team at the highest possible level. Even so, £100,000 in 1980 was a serious amount of money and to find oneself in the red to that extent was a sobering experience.

To make matters worse, we suddenly found ourselves with no oil and no tyre contract for 1981 when, just before Christmas, our previous sponsors, Castrol and Dunlop, decided to pull out. The days of the free rally tyre, it seemed, were over.

Jill had taken over as our Financial Director by now and, accompanied by our accountant and chief backer, Jim Dewar, she went to see Rothmans to try and find some way of sorting out the mess. I wasn't allowed anywhere near the meeting, having been told very firmly to go away and get on with running the team and to leave the financial side to others.

After being locked in a room with the Rothmans people for about five days, Jill and Jim emerged with a completely new deal whereby Rothmans very generously agreed to write off the £120,000 they had already paid in advance for the 1981 season to bail us out for the previous year. They also came to the rescue with additional budget for tyres, which were eventually supplied by Pirelli, while Duckhams later came in to help with the oil and other support. As a result of this renegotiation, and with Jill now keeping a very tight hold on the purse strings, we were able to turn that £100,000 loss into a £100,000 profit in 1981.

In the meantime, there had also been significant changes to the Team in the run-up to the new season. Ari and David Richards would still be leading our attack on the World Championship but, sadly, we had lost Hannu, who had joined Audi Sport on a full time basis to spearhead their World Championship challenge in the awesome Quattro. To replace him and to give us an additional third option, we introduced two new drivers in Pentti Airikkala and Malcolm Wilson.

I chose Pentti because, in previous years, he had won every round of the British Championship at some time or another and would therefore bring enormous experience to the Team. David Richards nominated Malcolm Wilson, now in charge of the Ford World Rally Team, because he felt it would be good for our image to be seen giving a helping hand to a young British driver.

Looking back now at the programme for that season, I can't believe that we agreed to take it on. I certainly wouldn't do so now. The contract stipulated that we had to prepare thirty-five cars to be entered in twenty events – ten in the World Championship, five in the British Open Championship and five in the Mediterranean. To the best of my knowledge, that is a feat that had never been undertaken by the largest Works teams. And it was all done on what was a shoestring compared with modern day budgets.

Against this background, and with Ari hurling himself into the fray with his customary abandon – his progress through the events soon conforming to the familiar crash-win-crash-win pattern that had our regular body shell suppliers, Gartrac, working overtime – the story of our assault on the World Championship, in particular, gradually developed into an epic adventure during which we rode a roller coaster of triumph and disaster.

There were many times during that extraordinary year when we wondered whether we would actually be able to see it through to the finish. That we were eventually able to do so owed much to the incredible team spirit that built up along the way, more than making up for our lack of numbers and resources compared to most of our Factory rivals.

Things got off to an inauspicious start, our single entry interest in the Monte Carlo ending abruptly when Ari's engine expired. Fortunately, our next outing restored some of our confidence as Pentti, with his new co-driver, Phil Short, making his first-ever appearance in a professional team, romped home well ahead of the field in the Mintex Rally.

Our good form continued in Sweden, with Ari and Pentti finishing 2nd and 3rd respectively behind Hannu – who pointed the way to the future with the first victory for a 4x4 car in his Audi Quattro – only for disaster then to strike twice in a row. Both cars crashed in Portugal, although not in quite such spectacular fashion as in the previous year, and morale plummeted even further when they both had to retire on the Circuit of Ireland.

Due to Ari's enormous popularity in England, it had always been intended that he should make at least one appearance in the British Championship and, having chosen the Welsh Rally, he duly raised our spirits again with a comprehensive victory. We received a further, rather unexpected boost when Pentti, who had been entered in the Costa Smeralda and Elba rallies purely for Rothmans marketing purposes, proceeded to come 2nd and 4th and, as a result, suddenly found himself leading the European Championship.

With our British and World Championship points positions not quite as healthy as we would have liked at this point, there was a great debate as to whether we should maybe drop the British Championship altogether in favour of concentrating on the European. At the very least I felt that we should continue with both, thereby adding another string to our bow. Rothmans, however, chose instead to abandon the European Championship, a decision I have always regretted.

We next returned to Greece to defend our famous victory of the previous year and this time I increased our support team from sixteen to twenty-one, much to the amusement of the other World Championship contenders, who still could not believe that it was possible to run two cars efficiently with such a small crew. Once again, we were able to leave them shaking their heads in bemused admiration as Ari came up trumps, although it has to be conceded that our success on this occasion was largely due to Audi's unfortunate and controversial disqualification on a technicality relating to a special cooling system operated through the headlamps.

By that point in the event, Hannu had already provided a impressive demonstration of his own special genius, getting his mechanics to disconnect part of the four-wheel-drive transmission after having problems with the differential and yet still managing to maintain his lead in what had thus become a front-wheel drive car. A fire that started when fuel was spilled over the Audi's over-heated exhaust, and which left Team Manager Walter Treser quite badly burned, added further drama to an event that I'm sure Hannu would prefer to forget.

Our seesawing fortunes brought us down to earth once more in Argentina, where an accident put us out of contention, only for hopes to be raised again with an outright victory for Ari in Brazil. This came after I had persuaded Rothmans to pay for a spare car to be rushed out from England to replace the one wrecked in Argentina. At the same time, we had entered a second car in both events for Domingo de Vita, a private client who not only brought much-needed funds into the Team but also gave us the benefit of his local knowledge and experience.

Back in Europe, Ari surprised us all again with a tremendous victory in the 1000 Lakes Rally. I remember thinking at the time that this was undoubtedly one of the greatest milestones in Ari's career and the key turning point for all of us that season. Winning this Blue Riband event in such convincing style seemed to give Ari a new self-assurance and ensured that we moved on from Jyväskylä with morale sky high.

Two consecutive victories had enabled us make up the ground lost during our rather shaky start to the season and leaving us now lying just six points behind Guy Frequelin, now boss of the Citroen World Rally Team, in his Talbot Sunbeam Lotus.

Partnered by Jean Todt, Guy had driven very carefully and very skilfully throughout and was a constant threat to us.

Tension was mounting as rallying's travelling circus pitched camp in San Remo and prepared for the next round of the Championship and it was now that I and David Richards had another major row over tactics, one that has been the subject of heated discussion ever since.

The last night of San Remo in those days was similar to Monte Carlo, with a mountain loop that took about eight hours. At this point we were a mere 34 seconds behind leader Michele Mouton in her Audi Quattro. Ari, as usual, wanted to go all out for glory whereas David thought that in the circumstances - and given the overall points situation - it wasn't worth the risk and that we would be better off to go easy and settle for a comfortable 2nd place.

After much discussion, I sided with Ari. Blindingly quick, he was always a potential winner and our thinking was that if we really went for it on the first special stage of that section, which was about 50km long, we might then be in a position to put pressure on Michele, with a decent chance of snatching a really decisive victory. If, on the other hand, we had not been able to make any impression by then, we would be far enough ahead of the rest of the field to relax and settle for a safe 2nd place and the points.

Of course, the worst happened. Ari crashed, arrived at the service point with punctured tyres and a broken suspension that needed considerable repair work and ended up as a result in 7th place overall. Sitting in their posh new motor home near the finishing ramp,the Rothmans management were understandably disappointed by this unhappy outcome and I found myself facing a rather grim-faced welcoming committee who, led by David, charged me with making a bad decision that could damage our Championship hopes.

I have to say that I remain unapologetic to this day. I hold the view that in rallying, as in any sport and as in life generally, there are some people who are born winners. Vatanen was one of them and I was not going to deprive him of the opportunity of another outright World Championship victory for the sake of 34 seconds. I felt that we had to give it our best shot but on this occasion it simply didn't work out. I made a similar decision some years later with David Llewellin on the Scottish Rally and it worked brilliantly. Then, of course, I was showered with accolades from the sponsors.

Any Team manager will tell you that being locked into a closely contested Championship battle can turn into a mathematical nightmare once you have to start calculating how to wring the maximum points advantage out of any given situation, adjusting your strategy accordingly. Most drivers, if they are honest, will tell you that they much prefer to try and win a rally outright rather than play it safe and go for position. Either way, it's always a bit of a gamble. As it turned out, Frequelin had to retire on the San Remo so, even with his distant 7th place, Ari had closed the gap to a mere two points.

At this point Rothmans sat down and decided to fund an extra entry in the Ivory Coast Rally in West Africa in an attempt to gain a few extra points that would put us in pole position for the last event of the season, the Lombard RAC Rally.

This was a prospect that didn't thrill me at all. I have never been a great fan of African rallies because, quite apart from the unpredictable hazards to life and limb that you are always likely to encounter in regions where there is no real car culture, I simply can't see the point of events in which the cars are invariably reduced to a pile of twisted scrap metal.

You can do more damage in a three-day African rally than in a 23-day London-Mexico marathon and the costs are often four to five times that of a regular event. You know before you start that the chances are there will be nothing left of the car by the end, that the engine will have been wrecked along with the transmission, the differential, the suspension and the underfloor of the body shell. It's all about the masochistic satisfaction of being able to say that you made it to the finish line.

The Ivory Coast Rally is the worst of them all as far as I am concerned and should never have been included in the World Championship. Everything that is bad about African rallying is magnified on the Bandama event, where, on one famous occasion in 1972, only two cars managed to finish - and they were both out of time! When Ari almost immediately crashed head-on into a truck that was trundling merrily along the rally route, I really thought that his Championship title was going to slip away.

Somehow we managed to keep the tired and battered Escort going as it gradually started to disintegrate along the way. We were slipping further and further behind the rest of the field as the penalties started to be calculated in hours rather than minutes, but it became essential to complete the course if only to boost flagging Team morale. More than on any other event with which I have ever been involved, we were like men on a mission.

Operating out of two dilapidated ex-Godfrey Davis hire vans that I'd got hold of for the event, both of which had gone twice round the clock before they even got there, our mechanics struggled on heroically, tracking the ailing car through jungle and desert scrub while I,together with Phil Short, masterminded operations from a light aircraft overhead.

At one point the clutch started to go, but, having stopped to change it on the side of a forest road in the middle of a pitch black African night, they got the gearbox out only to find that the spare clutch was the wrong sort. There was nothing for it but to put the old one back and soldier on as best they could. During this operation the car fell off its axle stands, narrowly avoiding serious injury to the mechanic who was underneath at the time.

And so it went on. A broken half shaft, a snapped alternator bracket, a seized wheel bearing – the car was literally falling to pieces, with David Richards at one point having to operate the windscreen wipers by hand with a piece of string. There is a scene in the video of the event in which David, unable any longer even to get his door open, is seen climbing out of the window of the trashed car, urging the mechanics on to yet another effort.

We eventually managed to limp over the finishing ramp, the last of just nine cars out of fifty-one starters that made it through to the end. Almost unbelievably, we were a full day behind winners Timo Salonen and Seppo Harjanne in a Datsun, and yet we still managed to pick up a couple of points. All this time later I think I can now safely reveal that the event cost us £100,000 and I do wonder whether, at £50,000 per point, it was really worth it.

What it did achieve was to set up the most exciting possible climax to the World Championship. With Ari and Frequelin now dead level on points, it was going to go right down to the wire and everything would be settled on the very last event. I decided to prepare a brand new car for Ari in order to give him the best possible chance and, as the teams assembled in Chester for the start of the Lombard RAC, the atmosphere was electric.

Hannu Mikkola won it, dominating from start to finish in his Audi Quattro, but Ari produced one of the most mature drives of his career to finish 2nd, while Frequelin's challenge faded away when he again had to retire. Pentti came in a very commendable 4th while poor Malcolm Wilson, who had had no luck at all during the whole campaign, again failed to finish.

Our final tally for the year was five outright victories, including three in the World Championship, four 2nd spots and, of course, the coveted World Driver's Championship title for Ari. It would have been nice if the story could have ended on that triumphant note, instead of which there was a twist in the tale that came as even more of a shock than the previous year's revelation of our £100,000 loss.

On the eve of that climactic final event I happened to be with a senior Rothmans manager, watching as Ari was presented with an Italian motorsport magazine's Driver Of The Year Award and

David picked up his Golden Halda Award as Co-Driver Of The Year, when we were joined by Ford's Peter Ashcroft, who then proceeded to knock us all sideways with some completely unexpected news. We listened in stunned silence as he revealed that the launch of the new, much vaunted Ford rally car that we had been awaiting so eagerly for the previous two years and that we thought was going to be ready in time for the next season, had now been postponed indefinitely.

For both Rothmans and David Sutton Cars this was a real body blow. After all, one of the main reasons for investing so much time, effort and money in the existing car was the promise of an exciting new car, which was understood to be just around the corner. The Rothmans budget for 1981 alone was £1.3 million, with almost no contribution from Ford themselves – Rothmans even paid all the drivers' and co-drivers' fees – and I know for a fact that some of their senior executives felt let down by the abrupt change of plan. On top of everything else, Ford decided not to advertise or publicise our World Championship triumph because we had done it with an old-style Escort that was no longer available to the general public.

It was a rather sorry end to what had been a great adventure. To this day, I have never received so much as a letter of congratulation from Ford for helping them to win the Drivers' World Championship, let alone a modest lunch. And when, some years later, they threw a special party to celebrate 30 years of rallying with the Ford Escort, they forgot to invite me. Never mind. I have the consolation of knowing that despite all the money they have poured into their Works Teams in the years since then, they have never managed to win the World Championship again. And I very much doubt whether any private Team will ever get the chance to repeat our achievement.

Rothmans, meanwhile, were much more gracious and showed their gratitude for our efforts by presenting me with a very handsome Dunhill watch and a cheque for £25,000. I gave £1000 to each of the mechanics and used what was left to treat myself to a Princess 32 motor cruiser, which Jill and I kept moored down on the South coast but rarely got time to use in what turned out to be the even busier years ahead.

On a very private note, my delight at our success was tinged with sadness that my mother had not lived to witness my greatest triumph. She had been diagnosed with ovarian cancer but, characteristically, kept the true severity of the situation from me at first because she didn't want to upset me. She was eventually admitted to hospital and on June 19th, 1981, shortly after returning from the Acropolis Rally, I received a phone call at five o'clock in the morning, advising me that her condition had suddenly deteriorated and urging me to go in as quickly as possible. I didn't waste a second but, unfortunately, by the time I got there it was all over.

Like all of us with busy careers that keep us constantly on the move, I regretted afterwards that I had not made a greater effort to give her more of my time. I had kept in touch mostly with postcards from wherever I happened to be in the world, all of which she kept in a scrapbook, along with newspaper and magazine cuttings charting my career. It turned out that from the moment I left Nottingham and moved down to London she had been going out to buy Motoring News to see if there were any articles about me, carefully cutting out and filing any rally report in which my name was mentioned. It was only when I had to go through her things after her death and found the scrapbook that I realised quite what a close interest she had taken in my activities.

She was a very sweet person - but also very proud. It gave me great satisfaction to be able to buy her a house once things started to go well for me and to help her financially in other ways, but I always had to be very secretive about the way I paid some of the household bills, getting the utility companies to send the bills direct to me, for instance.

Mum was not at all comfortable with the idea of being a kept woman and if I ever discreetly left a £10 note on the mantlepiece she would make a point of returning it to me. I owed everything to her, including that first job at Beardall's that she fixed up for me and that led to everything else I have ever done. I just wish she could have lived to paste the reports of my World Championship triumph into her scrap album.

There was a more light-hearted postscript to that momentous year. While we had won the Drivers' Championship with Ari and David, Talbot had taken the Manufacturers' title, making it one of the few occasions on which the Championship has been split. It had been a thrilling contest, undertaken in a very good spirit, and, as we fought it out around the world, we had all got to know each other really well, with quite a few of the mechanics, especially, becoming good mates.

When it was all over, there was a lot of good-natured banter about who were the *real* World Champions and it was decided to organise a football match to settle the issue. Rothmans and Talbot Team T-shirts were duly produced, a venue was arranged and everybody got very involved. Unfortunately, I have to report that on the day Talbot totally annihilated us, the final score being something like 11-2. It seems that as a Team Manager I should maybe stick to rallying. When it comes to soccer, I am clearly no Alex Ferguson! Still, it was a nice bit of end-of-term fun before we all went our separate ways

In many respects 1981 seemed to mark the end of an era in rallying. A new breed of powerful, turbo-charged, four-wheel drive cars was starting to make its presence felt. In terms of personnel, too, there were some significant changes. Jean Todt and David Richards both used that year's RAC as their driving swansong, Jean Todt moving into management with Peugeot before going on later to take charge of Ferrari's Formula 1 Team, while David also moved behind the scenes to start laying the foundations of his spectacular career as the Bernie Ecclestone of rallying.

For David, it was the perfect opportunity to retire on a high. Apart from that, I suspect that the somewhat hair-raising experience of co-driving with Ari had finally started to take its toll. They had been involved in some fairly serious accidents in those last two seasons – head-on into the truck on the Ivory Coast, through a bridge parapet and down into the river thirty feet below in Monte Carlo and rolling through a steeply terraced vineyard in Portugal, to mention just a few of the more spectacular prangs. Now, with a young family to consider, I think that David felt it was the right time to remove himself from the firing line. As he later admitted to me: "There comes a time when you have to realise that you're only mortal."

For Ari himself, that realisation was to come a couple of years later with the horrific accident in Argentina from which he barely emerged alive. Argentina was always one of the fastest events - it was in that same year that Stig Blomqvist recorded an average speed of over 189 kph on the first stage - and Ari was going at full tilt when his Peugeot dug its nose in on a jump and cartwheeled, end-over-end. His co-driver, Tony Harriman, escaped relatively unscathed but Ari, whose seat broke loose, was so seriously injured that it was touch-and-go for a time and he spent weeks in hospital. He never won another Championship event after that, concentrating on long-distance rallies before eventually retiring and going into politics as a Finnish member of the European Parliament.

Rothmans, meanwhile, took their sponsorship to Opel in Germany following the Ford bombshell and I took David Sutton Cars to Audi. On the back of our World Championship triumph where else could we go but forward with the new technology?

QUATTROMANIA

At the headquarters of Audi Sport in Ingolstadt, in December 1981, I found myself, for the second time in my life, being asked by the senior managers of a major manufacturer to leave a boardroom meeting and wait outside in the corridor like a naughty schoolboy while they discussed my fate. And, once again, it was to be a key turning point in my career.

Under consideration were the provisional costings I had given Audi Sport UK for the 1982 British Championship. Half an hour later I was called back in to the meeting and was both relieved and flattered to be told: "We can't really afford you, but you are the best in the business so we will find the money from somewhere." As an added bonus, I was delighted to be further informed that they had also successfully negotiated with Audi Germany to acquire the services of Hannu Mikkola for our formative year.

I should explain that this new deal had not come completely out of the blue. Some months before, Audi had visited Rothmans in Aylesbury to discuss the possibility of Rothmans becoming the main Audi sponsor for the 1982 season and beyond. Not many people knew about that meeting, but David Richards and I had been flown back from South America especially to attend it and although nothing came of the discussions that took place, I was able to make close contact with the Audi people as a result.

At this distance I think I can also safely confess that Audi had actually leased a Ford Escort from us during the 1981 season so that they could do detailed comparison tests with a proven rally winner. So, one way and another, the groundwork had already been laid by the time Ford suddenly left us all in the lurch and in urgent need of a new partner.

Once the deal with Audi had been signed and sealed on December 17th, 1981, things started to happen very quickly indeed. The ink was hardly dry on the contract before my mechanics were rushed to Ingolstadt to start preparing for the first event of the new season. This was then just eight weeks away, with Christmas in between, but, on February 15th, we duly arrived in Yorkshire for the Mintex Rally with what was to become the famous LYV 4X, having successfully created a completely new Team from scratch in what must have been close to record time.

We had also taken on a new identity. To avoid any confusion between the winding down of the Rothmans Ford operation and the formation of the new Audi Team we had decided to form a separate company called David Sutton Motorsport Limited to look after Audi exclusively.

This was as much for our own internal benefit as for the outside world because, with the situation having changed so rapidly, I still had the entire Rothmans Team to sell at this point and our workshop was packed with Ford Escorts, Ford service vans, spare parts, wheels, tyres and goodness knows what else – including the Ivory Coast cars and equipment, most of which, rather typically, had not found its way back to England until five months after the event!

In the end it was to take us fifteen months altogether to sell all this surplus gear, an enormous amount of capital to have lying around the place for so long. Normally, this might have caused financial headaches, but we were very fortunate insofar as the terms of the Audi deal meant that they owned all the hardware, including not just the rally cars themselves but the service vans, spare parts and support vehicles, so my capital involvement was quite small.

Despite having to do such a rush job to get everything ready in time for the start of the British Championship season, we won the Mintex in sensational style, with the added thrill of introducing 'Quattromania' to the UK. The advent of turbo-charged, four-wheel-drive cars had ushered in a new era of rally motorsport and it was tremendously exciting to be involved with Audi at the forefront of such an important development.

While we were still celebrating a brilliant start to our British Championship campaign, we found ourselves enjoying an unexpected little triumph elsewhere. 'My' World Champion, Ari Vatanen, had not been invited to join the Opel Team when Rothmans moved their sponsorship across and was thus left effectively unemployed for most of 1982. So, when he asked me if I could prepare a Ford Escort for him to drive in the Swedish Rally I felt I could hardly refuse. Ari went on to finish 2nd, just a few minutes behind Stig Blomqvist in the Swedish Audi Quattro – but well ahead of the Rothmans Opel driven by Walter Rohrl. The look on the faces of the Opel Team was wonderful to behold and must have given Ari particular satisfaction.

As Quattromania continued to spread, enquiries were coming in from drivers and teams all over the world. Everybody wanted to drive a Quattro and I had no problem finding a replacement for Hannu Mikkola at short notice when Audi Sport in Germany pulled rank over Audi Sport UK and exercised their contractual right to have first call on Hannu's services, commandeering him for the Corsica Rally and leaving us without a driver for the Welsh. I called up my old friend Bjorn Waldegard and he almost bit my hand off when I offered him the drive. So excited was he about the prospect of getting behind the wheel of a Quattro for the first time that he agreed to do it for a nominal fee. I couldn't quite afford his regular Swedish co-driver so I brought in Phil Short – the first of three drives with three different World Champions that I handed to Phil on a plate.

Needless to say, Bjorn came storming home – despite having problems with the suspension. My immediate boss, Audi Sport UK's John Mezaros, was so delighted with Bjorn's performance that he promptly insisted on topping up his driver's fee. I had been equally impressed with the Swede when I first worked with him some years previously, despite the fact that on that occasion he had to retire early after rolling the Eaton Yale Escort he was driving for us in the Scottish Rally. What won my respect was the way in which he conducted himself when he faced the Press immediately afterwards and was asked if the car had been all right. "Perfect," he replied. "I simply made a mistake." That sort of straightforward honesty was typical of this truly great driver and enormously charming personality.

By this time we were completely at home with the Quattro, winning the confidence of the Factory in Germany to such an extent that they asked us to manage a second car on their behalf. Our brief was to complete the Italian Championship with the talented but wildly erratic Michel Cinotto. This turned out to be a less than totally happy experience because, if the car didn't break of its own accord, then Cinotto would promptly drive it off the road and destroy it. The programme did, however, give us the opportunity to get closer to the Factory, not only adding a second string to our bow but also giving us another taste of the World Championship, since one of the events in the Cinotto programme was San Remo.

Hannu returned to the Team for the Scottish Rally, which he won at a canter, giving us our third victory of the year. Soon after this, another very pleasant surprise came our way when the Factory invited us to supervise and manage a two-car entry in the New Zealand and Brazilian World Championship events.

I was quite astonished that after only six months working experience with the Quattro we should be entrusted with such a heavy responsibility, a vote of confidence that was extremely gratifying. We were quickly brought down to earth in New Zealand,where both cars had to retire with mechanical problems, but our luck changed dramatically in Brazil when the amazing Michele Mouton scored a sensational victory, coming home an incredible thirty minutes ahead of second-placed Walter Rohrl in the Rothmans Opel.

This was the second time that year that a Team under private management had beaten the Rothmans Opel, something that must have been hard for both sponsor and manufacturer to swallow. Rothmans, in particular, had clearly decided that they would get a better deal with a Factory than they would with a private Team and it must have been very galling for them to have to accept that this was not necessarily the case.

At the end of the season Hannu returned to Factory team duty for the Lombard RAC Rally, in which the other Works Quattro was to be driven by Michele Mouton, and that left us, once again, searching for a stand-in. There had been a lot of pressure throughout the year for Audi Sport UK to show the flag by engaging a British driver so we decided to offer our Quattro to Malcolm Wilson, with journalist Mike Greasley in the co-driver's seat.

In addition, the Factory had asked us to look after three other cars in the event, driven by Harald Demuth, John Buffum and Lassi Lampi. This presented us with something of a logistical nightmare, not least because all four cars were running on different tyres, making the loading plan for the service vans, alone, extremely complicated. One way and another, we had our plates very full but managed to come away with a Top Ten finish for Malcolm, giving ourselves the satisfaction of knowing that we had done our bit for a British driver.

Audi had nominated the following season as that in which Hannu was to make his bid for the World Championship, meaning that a permanent replacement had to be found for us. I couldn't have been more delighted when the Factory then informed us that we were to be given Stig Blomqvist.

I had not previously worked with Stig, but I knew him by reputation as a man of enormous talent and few words. This proved to be absolutely spot-on. Thanks to him, we enjoyed an amazingly successful year, winning every round of the British Championship except two, giving Audi their first-ever tarmac victory on the Ulster Rally and rounding things off in truly grand style by coming home first in the Lombard RAC, ahead of the Works Team. Despite all this, I never felt that I really knew

Stig. At the service points, my solicitous enquiries as to whether everything was OK would invariably be met by a one-word "yes" or "no" answer, followed, if anything wasn't quite right, by a terse summing up of the problem. He would then jump back in the car and roar off to set another string of fastest times.

One of the few failures during that fantastic year was on the Isle of Man and, as luck would have it, this was the event at which the Managing Director of Audi Sport UK, Michael Heelas, opted to make his one and only rally appearance. He joined me in the management car to follow our progress in what we confidently expected to be yet another triumph, only for the Quattro's engine to blow itself to smithereens. At that point Michael decided that he was perhaps a bad omen and we never saw him again over the next few years.

Hannu Mikkola, meanwhile, had crowned a wonderful year for Audi by duly becoming the 1983 World Champion. It was to be Stig's turn for a crack at the title in 1984, but, just as we were resigning ourselves to the idea of having to go off yet again in search of a replacement, Hannu confided in me that he was looking forward to a slightly quieter year and would welcome a return to the British Championship. This was a fantastic bonus not just for the Team but for me personally, as Hannu had by now become a close friend.

He got us off to a flying start by winning the Mintex Rally, by now rather ironically renamed The National Breakdown Rally in deference to its new sponsor. At Easter, Hannu returned briefly to the Factory Team for the Safari Rally and I decided that his place on the Circuit of Ireland Rally should be taken by Harald Demuth. Harald, by this time, was making a big name for himself with Audi in the German Championship but, unfortunately, he lasted only two days in Ireland before being forced out with engine trouble.

Hannu was back in time for the Welsh Rally, and his customary place in the winner's enclosure, before then going on to win the Scottish Rally by the quite staggering margin of six minutes.

Arne Hertz, his regular co-driver for many years, was not available for this event, having been sent off to New Zealand by Audi for other duties, and this opened the way for me to give Phil Short his second opportunity to partner a World Champion.

The Ulster Rally then produced a rallying sensation that is still being talked about in Ireland to this day. Audi had selected Ulster as one of the tarmac events where they could test the awesome and newly arrived Audi Sport Quattro. With a massive 550 bhp, this was by far the most powerful rally car that the world had seen so far and was the centre of attention wherever it appeared, for drivers and public alike. I had never in my life before seen drivers at the start of a special stage leave their own cars to watch a rival competitor off the ramp as they did that time in Ireland. With two-foot-long flames shooting out the back, this monster scorched a trail of four black tyre marks onto the road wherever it went and was truly a sight to behold.

We were greatly flattered to have a prototype model under our management and, with Hannu away driving in Argentina, it was Walter Rohrl who took over behind the wheel in Ulster, totally annihilating the opposition to give us our second tarmac victory with a Quattro. For some reason, Walter had a reputation for being rather difficult, but I have to say that I found him absolutely charming, perfectly polite and extremely co-operative in every way. Hannu returned to the Team to drive a similar monster for the last round of the Championship on the Isle of Man but, disappointingly, had to retire with gearbox failure after just a few hours.

At this time, Audi Sport UK also sponsored the last round of the British National series and usually obliged the organisers by sending along either a star driver or a celebrity co-driver. On this occasion we recruited Michele Mouton, with Pauline Gullick as co-driver, and, as ever, Michele kept the men very much on their toes, eventually coming in 2nd, just a minute behind winner Malcolm Wilson in his privately entered Quattro.

The year ended on a satisfactory note when Hannu secured

2nd place in the Lombard RAC Rally, a mere forty-one seconds behind winner Ari Vatanen. And this despite opting to drive the same A2 Quattro in which Stig had won the event the previous year – and which now has pride of place in our Historic Motorsport Museum at Daventry – rather than the more powerful Sport model that had been entered by the Factory.

In between the British Championship events of that season, we were also given the task of managing a small European Programme for the talented but ebullient and often very noisy American John Buffum. Funded by his faithful, long-time sponsor, BFGoodrich, John had a year of mixed fortunes. His 5th on the Acropolis was an excellent result, an outright win in Cyprus was even better and he would have been the first American to gain a coveted 'A' seeding had he not rolled his car on the last night of the RAC.

A busy year saw two other interesting developments for David Sutton Motorsport. Firstly, the Rothmans Ford assets had long been sold on and it would be true to say that the money was starting to burn a large hole in my pocket. Mindful of the fact that I could not necessarily expect to stay in motorsport forever and therefore on the lookout for a suitable alternative investment opportunity, I jumped at the chance to acquire a small Audi Volkswagen dealership in Dunchurch, near Rugby, in Warwickshire.

Secondly, World Championship events were now, increasingly, being controlled from the air rather than on the ground, this being the only way to ensure clear, reliable and unbroken radio contact between Team and driver, so when Audi offered me their aircraft contract, I flew immediately to America with Phil Short to complete the purchase of a pressurised twin-engine Cessna 340 aircraft ready for the start of the new season.

I flew back from the States in a relaxed mood, with everything seemingly well under control but, as John Lennon once so perceptively remarked, life is what happens to you when you're making other plans and 1985 soon turned into a non-stop catalogue of disaster on almost every front.

It all started to go horribly wrong when the aircraft that I had just bought at great expense suffered an engine failure on the way over from America and was grounded in Greenland. By the time a replacement engine had been flown out along with a specialist mechanic to supervise the fitting, we were already another £40,000 out of pocket before we'd even taken delivery! What's more, we were left without an aircraft for the first two events of the season while we waited for the Cessna to arrive and so, in order to fulfil our contract, we had to find and hire an alternative plane, adding further to the unexpected extra costs.

We were still reeling from this when a letter from our landlords dropped on my desk, informing me that the rent on our London workshop was about to be increased by a swingeing 200%. This nasty little shock finally convinced me that the time had come to move out of London, but that was easier said than done at a time when commercial rents everywhere were spiralling. It also involved the added distraction of looking for somewhere that would be both suitable and affordable.

The good news, meanwhile, was that our main driver for 1985 was the formidable Michele Mouton, without any doubt the best woman driver in rally history and more than a match for even the best male drivers, a fact that she quite clearly proved with her success at World Championship level, including two outright victories. As even the likes of Ari Vatanen and Hannu Mikkola will attest, Michele was in a class of her own compared to any other female driver there has ever been before or since, including Pat Moss at her peak.

Part of the secret of her success was that, with the wholehearted encouragement of her father, Michele had started driving competitively at a very young age and was obviously blessed with great natural talent. But what really set her apart was her attitude. Although very feminine most of the time, she became a changed character once she got behind the wheel, when the aggression, the determination and the sheer strength that she brought to her driving could be quite fearsome. In rallying as in everyday life, men tend to be very rude about woman drivers – but nobody was ever rude about Michele.

The big Group B Audis were extremely heavy cars, with endless complex controls and switches that together demanded not only physical strength from the driver but also a very quick-thinking and energetic technique. That Michele was so easily able to handle them is a further tribute to her skills.

We were able to run a second car that season and perhaps it was Michele's presence in the lead car that scared off the first two drivers we approached. It was certainly unusual for anyone at that time to refuse the opportunity of driving one of the magic Quattros. So I was very surprised when both British Champion Mark Lovell and the glamorous Louise Aitken-Walker turned us down. But, as things turned out, I was rather pleased that they did because it opened the way for David Llewellin. Pirelli's Andy Hallam suggested David, who not only leapt at the chance but also turned out to be a brilliantly talented driver and a charming character for whom I developed enormous respect.

We got off to a disappointing start in the opening event when both our cars had to retire, leaving Malcolm Wilson to coast home in his privately entered Quattro. For the next event, Michele was offered the Audi Sport Quattro and it was then that I came to suspect that the British Championship was being used by the Factory as a test bed for the development of the car. Michele was actually leading when forced to retire and the best that David could manage was a distant 8th.

Our fortunes improved slightly on the Welsh Rally. Although Malcolm again won convincingly in his private Quattro, Michele was right behind him in 2nd place with David finishing 4th. But while Malcolm continued his winning ways on the Scottish, both our cars again failed to last the distance.

Frustratingly, Michele was only a few seconds off the lead when she had to retire with a gearbox problem that, in my opinion, could and should have been avoided. Here was another example of a wrong decision by a Team manager that possibly cost us the event.

What happened on this occasion was that, at a particular service point, Michele asked me if we could change the gearbox. I readily agreed and arranged for this to be done. However, my decision was then over-ruled by the Factory engineer from Germany who was with the Team at the time to keep an official eye on the Audi Sport Quattro. He insisted that a change of oil was all that was needed and I had no choice but to go along with the Factory's advice, against my better judgement. Three stages later the gearbox blew and Michele was left stranded in the forest.

On the Ulster Rally, both Malcolm and Michele retired and the best we could manage was 4th place with David Llewellin. As we then prepared for the Manx, the final event of the British Championship, the mathematical calculations revealed that at least three drivers were in with a chance of winning the title, including Malcolm.

We reported this to the Factory, who co-operated by allowing us to run no less than four Quattros in the event, the object of the exercise being to try and ensure that Audis filled as many as possible of the top three or four places, thus forcing the other leading contenders into lower point-scoring positions. They provided Michele with the S1 Sport Quattro and generously loaned Malcolm the earlier Sport Quattro, while David Llewellin and Harald Demuth were allocated our regular A2 models.

Talk about the best-laid plans of mice and men - and Rally Team managers! Despite all our careful plotting, the event turned into an utter disaster when both Michele and Malcolm had accidents and David retired with engine failure. Only Harald managed to finish, coming in a lowly 4th. To add to the frustration, Malcolm had been leading comfortably until he made the mistake that led to one of the biggest and most spectacular accidents ever suffered by a Quattro.

It happened as he came over a humpback bridge that routinely produced quite a big jump. The moment that he took off, Malcolm realised instantly that he had come into the bridge too fast and that, as a result, he was going to land close to the corner sixty yards beyond. To allow for this he started to put a bit of lock on in mid-air, but that meant that when he did come down to earth he just nibbled at a stone wall at the side of the road and that was enough to send the car into orbit.

What followed was described by Per Eklund, who witnessed it at close quarters, as "a full Formula 1 accident". What remained of the car when the dust finally cleared was fit only for a plastic bag, with the wreckage strewn over a considerable distance and the camshaft found 100 yards away from the rest of the engine. Miraculously, Malcolm himself was able to walk away from this scene of utter devastation completely unhurt.

His was not the only lucky escape that weekend. On the second day, Audi executives John Mezaros, Steve Bagnall and Peter Cover were watching the event from a helicopter when the machine suddenly went out of control and into a steep dive. It was only at the very last second, with the stricken aircraft less than 200ft from the ground, that the ex-RAF pilot somehow managed to regain control and landed safely. Understandably, his passengers were extremely shaken. They had been absolutely convinced that they were about to die, to the extent that two of them actually shook hands and said goodbye to each other.

As we all retreated from the Isle of Man in a mood of deep depression, I found myself daring to hope that, surely, that must be it – that there couldn't possibly be any more shocks and disappointment in store for me before the end of what had already become one of the worst years in my entire motorsport career. Wrong!

At Austin Rover, during the latter part of 1985, John Davenport had been busy preparing for an assault on the World Championship the following year with the ill-fated Metro 6R4 and, helped by two well-connected advisers, he set about buying the crème de la crème of British rallying talent. We at Audi Sport promptly lost five key people at a stroke – David Llewellin, Phil Short and three of our mechanics. As a small British Team we simply could not compete with the lure of a three-year Factory contract and the promise of a full-blown World Championship Programme.

I echo the words of Ford's Peter Ashcroft who said of John Davenport at the time: "He must have the keys to the British Exchequer!" He had certainly been given a massive budget because nearly every top Team, including Ford, lost personnel to him. Malcolm Wilson was another who signed up. Despite all this, Austin Rover failed to score a single Championship point until well towards the end of the 1986 season. The car, it turned out, was not quite what it was cracked up to be and, on top of that, John Davenport himself made some big strategic and tactical mistakes in my view, quite apart from the financial ones that eventually landed him in jail. One way and another it was rather a sad interlude that ended suddenly and ignominiously when the Team disbanded after just one year.

Among the unfortunate side effects of this episode as far as I was concerned was the fact that it seemed effectively to end David Llewellin's World Championship aspirations. Although he did go on later to win two British Championship titles with Toyota, also driving for Nissan and Vauxhall, he never really got another chance to fulfil his potential at the highest level. That's a great pity in my view because David was not only a very nice guy – polite, charming, considerate to all those around him and a great favourite with the mechanics – but also an outstanding driver who should have gone on to greater things. Dear Tony Pond, who died so tragically young in 2002, was someone else who never drove again after the Austin Rover debacle.

Despite my respect for David Llewellin, I decided as soon as I discovered that he would be moving to Austin Rover the following year that I would have to withdraw his entry from the 1985 Lombard RAC Rally. After all, there was no way that we were going to enhance his four-wheel-drive experience only to then hand him on a plate to Mr Davenport.

However, I did not feel that it was necessary to adopt quite such a stringent attitude towards his co-driver, Phil Short, and arranged for him to partner Walter Rohrl – the third World Champion that I had provided for him. They proceeded to have a massive accident after fifteen stages and Hannu fared little better when he retired with electrical problems after twenty-two special stages. For the first time in many years, Audi had failed to make the Top Three on the RAC, having to content themselves with the scant consolation of 4th place secured by Per Eklund in a privately entered car.

The final blow of this difficult year came when two of my dearest and most loyal employees – mechanic Ron Lumley and General Manager David Darvill – announced that they would not be moving with me to Daventry, where our new Audi Volkswagen Dealership and Motorsport was due to open in the New Year with the promise of a brighter start to 1986.

DESERT RAIDERS

It would be an exaggeration to say that bands were playing and that fireworks lit up the sky, but, certainly by Northamptonshire standards, the razzamatazz that accompanied the opening of the new David Sutton Audi Volkswagen Dealership and Motorsport Centre in Daventry was pretty impressive.

The local Council had laid on a helicopter to fly in various V.I.Ps and more than a thousand people turned up to watch as Hannu Mikkola stepped forward to cut the tape. This was the highlight of what was one of the happiest days of my life, providing welcome light relief after all the trials and tribulations of the previous few months. I was tremendously proud of the building, which I had designed myself and which I felt was a credit both to Audi Volkswagen and rallying in general.

I had been looking around for new premises from the moment that our landlords in West London decided to hit us with a 200% rent rise. My original intention was to find somewhere within a thirty or forty-mile radius of London but, in the end, the very generous incentives offered by Daventry District Council proved irresistible. Keen to attract the kind of commercial and industrial development that would enable Daventry to compete with the enterprise zones on the other side of the M1 corridor in places like Corby, Kettering and Wellingborough, they successfully tempted us with everything from cheap land deals and interest free loans to subsidised housing for our employees.

At the same time, Jill displayed the sort of hard-headed business sense that left me dazed with admiration as I enjoyed the rare pleasure of watching our bank manager turn to putty in her hands. You know you're on to a good thing when they offer you a cup of tea and then bring out the best green-and-white china with the little black horse on it! Up until then I'd always had to go cap-in-hand whenever I wanted to borrow a few bob. Now all of a sudden the manager was fawning all over us, saying how nice it was to see us and wanting to know what he could for us.

Jill, who had swept in looking a million dollars in the fur coat I'd bought for her on a trip to Finland for the 1000 Lakes Rally, wasted no time in seizing the initiative. "We're building a brand new car dealership and motorsport centre at a cost of £350,000. We're going to need some funding and we're thinking of giving you the business," she announced imperiously.

"Oh, well, I don't think that should be a problem," beamed the manager, without a moment's hesitation. And that, as I recall, was the end of the conversation. As the CEO, I just sat there not saying a word and looking somewhat spare. I couldn't believe it had been that easy. But these were the heady days of the booming mid-eighties economy when almost anything was possible and the banks were throwing money at anyone with a half-decent business proposition. I should add here that things were to be very different indeed when I next found myself sitting in that office, as will be revealed in a later chapter.

For the time being, however, everything seemed to be going our way as we celebrated the move into our handsome new premises and also the welcome return of Hannu to our Team by winning the opening event of the season in style. Driving the powerful Audi Sport Quattro, Hannu came home in the National Breakdown Rally just eleven seconds ahead of David Llewellin in his Metro 6R4.

David then turned the tables on us by winning the Circuit of Ireland, after we had been forced to retire with suspension failure, but Hannu bounced back straightaway with victory on the Welsh Rally, coming home a few seconds ahead of Jimmy McRae, father of Colin and Alister. David, meanwhile, was knocked out of the running by a monumental accident. Recorded on film, this has been shown time and time again on television and elsewhere, picked out of the archives every time a producer calls for footage of a really spectacular crash sequence.

Sadly, this event will forever be tragically associated in my mind with a much more devastating accident elsewhere that was to have far-reaching repercussions both for the sport generally and for me personally. It was during the day of scrutineering that I had the unpleasant duty of visiting Hannu in his hotel room to break the terrible news that his dear friend and fellow countryman, Henri Toivonen, had been killed while competing on the Corsica Rally. Henri's car crashed off the road at speed and exploded in flames, killing Henri and his co-driver, the American Sergio Cresto, instantly. This shocking incident had a major and immediate impact on World Rallying and within a matter of hours the whole of sport had been turned upside down.

Concern about the safety of the big Group B cars had been growing for some time. At up to 600 bhp, these super-powerful, aerodynamically enhanced, flame-snorting monsters were real crowd-pullers that had added a thrilling new dimension of excitement to the sport. At the same time, there was no doubt that they had brought an extra element of risk for both drivers and spectators alike, with fans flocking to watch them in ever greater and more uncontrollable numbers, many of them bent on getting as dangerously close to the action as possible.

This was when the silly, reckless fashion started for trying to touch the cars as they passed. Markku Alen was said to have made the sickening discovery of a severed finger stuck in his wing mirror at the end of one particular stage and Roger Clark and Tony Mason collected a camera by its strap in the same sort of way while going through Sherwood Forest in the RAC. Not for the last time, rallying had started to become a victim of its own popularity.

Shortly before the tragic events in Corsica, there had already been another horrific accident during the Portuguese Rally when a Ford RS 200 car driven by former Portuguese Champion

Joaquim 'Kim' Santos careered off the road and ploughed into the packed crowd, killing three people and injuring thirty more. The fact that this disaster took place in full view of the television cameras, to be featured prominently on TV news bulletins around the world, brought home the full horror of what had happened. Coming so soon afterwards, Henri's accident was the final straw and twenty-four hours later the FIA, fearing that something even worse could be just around the next corner, announced an immediate ban on the Group B cars.

Audi promptly decided to go one step further, coming to the conclusion that this was a sensible moment at which to withdraw from rallying altogether, before anyone was killed or injured in one of their cars. To my mind, they were guilty of over-reaction and I was stunned when I got a call from Brian Bowler, Sales and Marketing Director of Audi Sport UK, instructing me to withdraw Hannu's entry from the Scottish Rally, in which we were due to compete in a few weeks time.

Coming just twenty weeks after the Grand Opening of our new combined dealership and Motorsport Centre, this was a devastating blow. What was I going to do with a massive site and a staff of over fifty people, some of whom now, inevitably, faced redundancy? My first thought was to investigate the legal possibility of seeking further compensation for the loss of our rally programme, but my lawyers advised that, as a small company, we simply did not have the resources to pursue that option. As they explained, the practicalities in such a situation were that by the time you had got the other side into court, in the hope that a judge might listen to your case sympathetically, so much time would have elapsed that it would probably be too late and you would already have gone out of business.

I decided that I would have to lie low for a while and hope that something could be salvaged out of the new Group A rules that were being examined and discussed by the FIA. In the meantime, all we had to rely on for the rest of the season was a private rental drive on the Gunaydin Rally in Turkey and an entry on the Manx Rally, for which I once again recruited the services of Harald Demuth. Neither was particularly successful. We had a good lead in Turkey, until a mistake by the co-driver dropped us to 3rd place, and on the Isle of Man Harald retired with a gearbox problem. I also entered Harald for the RAC in our own Audi Sport Quattro, but that ended in failure when the engine exploded.

Apart from that, I managed to keep the mechanics reasonably busy restoring some old Quattros that I had purchased from the Factory, including four of the ultimate S1 versions. Only eighteen remained in existence after the Group B ban and among those I managed to get hold of was the one bearing the chassis number 001, which we only finished restoring fifteen years later, in 2001. The others were all sold on to various private collectors, including the late Tom Hammonds, who drove the one he bought from us very successfully in the British Hill Climb Championship for many years.

I have always used the restoration of historic cars as a very useful stopgap to fill quiet periods in the workshop schedule. I am constantly on the lookout for interesting examples of classic cars and, apart from those advertised in the motorsport magazines, I have at various times chanced upon 'buried treasure' in the form of valuable donor cars lying around, forgotten, in the most unlikely locations – under an apple tree in an overgrown corner of an orchard in California, in a farmyard shed in Wales and behind a pile of cardboard boxes in a garage in South Africa. Most have been sold on, but the more interesting ones are now in our Historic Motorsport Museum, where we now have a collection worth in excess of £3 million. More about that later.

The crisis sparked by the banning of Group B was eased when, as I had hoped, Audi changed their minds about quitting rallying altogether and came back with a British Championship programme for 1987 that was actually bigger and better than we had ever had in previous years. They were joined this time by 'big brother' Volkswagen, who asked me to prepare four VW Golf 16-valve cars, to be driven by representatives from England, Ireland, Scotland and Wales.

David Llewellin and Phil Short had rejoined Audi Sport UK following the premature demise of the Austin Rover 6R4 Team and for them we built a brand new Audi Coupe Quattro that conformed to the new Group 'A' regulations. They raised quite a few eyebrows by leading twenty-one stages of the opening event before David went off the road and retired. Fortunately, a second Coupe Quattro, driven by Sebastian Lindholm and supported by us, came 3rd overall, ensuring that Audi's Championship campaign got off to a reasonable start

Things were looking even better after the next event when Llewellin and Lindholm finished 2nd and 3rd respectively in our heavy, underpowered cars. Both Quattros were again among the points on the Welsh Rally, where Simon Davidson, who now drives the gravel note car for Richard Burns, had his second Top Ten result of the season.

The Scottish Rally saw David Llewellin coming in 1st, a mere eleven seconds ahead of Jimmy McRae who, frustratingly for him, had now finished 2nd in the Scottish five times in six years. I have to say that on this occasion our success was at least partly down to one of my better management decisions.

As we came into the last night, David was still about a minute behind Jimmy. We knew that the final stages would be dusty, but we also felt that David could be quicker than Jimmy on the night section, so I instructed him to throw caution to the winds and go flat out. If the quest for victory ended with an accident, well, there was a spare body shell back at the workshop and at least we would have given the event our best shot. Sebastian Lindholm had already retired so it was a case of all or nothing, but I thought it was worth the gamble. And this time it came off brilliantly, with David pipping Jimmy at the post, having pushed things to the limit.

We did not fare so well in Ireland, finishing well off the pace

Markku Alen (above) making his sensational RAC debut in 1973 when he came very close to winning on what was only his second outing outside Finland.

My first Works contract and my first ever international win came courtesy of Ari Vatanen and Peter Bryant in the 1977 Mintex Rally (right).

My first RAC Rally win followed in 1978 with Hannu Mikkola and Arne Hertz (below).

Champagne moments for Hannu and Arne (left) after their 1978 RAC win and for Roger Clark and Neil Wilson after Roger's last-ever International win in Cyprus in 1980.

Roger and the whole team before the Cyprus event, with Jill and I trying to get in on the act on the far right of the picture.

Celebrity moments as I am interviewed by TV sports presenter Dickie Davis after the RAC in 1978 and (below) pose with boxer Henry Cooper and 'Police Five' presenter Shaw Taylor for a publicity shot organised by Centre Hotels, our sponsors at the time.
Co-driver Howard Scott (2nd left) is the one getting an adoring glance from the Centre Girl with driver Chris Sclater on her left.

Blonde on Blond as Jill poses with DJ Jimmy Savile, who joined her as a celebrity co-driver on the 1973 Daily Mirror RAC Rally (above) and with co-driver Dilys Rogers before the 1972 Scottish Rally (right).

Jimmy Savile, now Sir Jimmy, spent most of his time in the car waving to the fans (left. He was mobbed at every time control and it was quite a relief to the organisers when the Ford Escort Mexico eventually retired with engine failure.

Jill's famous gold Benson and Hedges Escort that she drove in as part of rallying's first-ever four figure sponsorship deal.... and Ari Vatanen's 'Black Beauty', the tarmac Escort we built for him to drive in between his World Championship commitments.

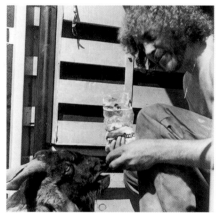

(Above) On parade with Rothmans Ford drivers (l to r) Ari Vatanen, Malcolm Wilson, Pentti Airikkala and the great Timo Makinen, drafted in to drive an extra car in the 1981 RAC Rally.

Pictured (right) with lunch companion in Argentina, John O'Connor is the best rally mechanic in the business as far as I am concerned.

John (third from right) with the rest of the workshop team.

Pentti Airikkala (above) on his way to an amazing 2nd place in the 1976 1000 Lakes, despite running on tyres that cost £8 each.

Pentti's wife, Kirsti, was the co-driver when Jill came home best of British in Finland's Arctic Rally (left) while (below) Jill is pictured 'flying' on the Donegal Rally with Pauline Gullick in the co-driver's seat.

Receiving a special award for Services to Finnish Sport at the end of the 1000 Lakes, with (l to r) Pentti Airikkala, Simo Lampinen, Markku Alen, Ari Vatanen and Matt Johansson.

And (below) giving a last minute team talk to the lads before the soccer match organised between Rothmans Ford, who won the 1981 Driver's World Championship and Talbot, who took the Manufacturer's title, to decide the overall winner. I'm obviously no Alex Ferguson - we got thrashed!

in 8th and 10th positions, and there was further disappointment on the Isle of Man, where we simply could not match the pace of the Ford Sierra Cosworths. The real surprise there was when Simon Davison came in 4th overall in the Golf GTi, well ahead of David in the Quattro. For that event, Sebastian Lindholm had also switched to a Golf and he just managed to scrape into the Top Ten.

Altogether, the Golfs had an amazing year and, despite many retirements and a series of accidents in which they consumed about six body shells between them, it nevertheless proved to be an interesting exercise.

In the midst of all this I enjoyed a welcome break from the usual routine when Audi asked me to escort a journalist and photographer to Pike's Peak in Colorado, where they were to work on preparing a magazine feature about one of America's most famous motorsport events, focusing on the attempt to set a new record for the twelve-mile hill climb in an S1. I took with me John Queenborough, a long-time rally enthusiast and an old friend whom I had brought in to supervise the construction of our new dealership and who then became the Service Manager there. With its summit 14,000 feet up in the Rockies, Pike's Peak provides a spectacular setting for what is a thrilling event and John and I came back suitably impressed.

Next, as a pat on the back for his efforts with the Quattro, we decided to give David a drive in the Cyprus Rally and he duly rewarded us with victory by a massive eleven minutes. Again, this success was marred for me by news of another tragic and fatal accident elsewhere. This time it was Henry Liddon who had died, not in a car but as a result of an air crash while he was attending the Ivory Coast Rally as co-ordinator for Toyota. Also a victim of the same accident was Malcolm Wilson's co-driver, Nigel Harris.

A wonderful character and a much respected figure in rallying, Henry was perhaps best remembered as Timo Mäkinen's co-driver. I had the privilege of working with him on several occasions, most memorably when I brought him in to partner Markku Alen for Markku's first ever drive outside Finland.

David, in a Coupe Quattro, rounded off the year with a respectable 6th overall in the RAC, while the amazing Kenneth Erikson came to drive our Golf and did extremely well to secure 9th position. I was hugely impressed by Kenneth's reaction on arriving at our workshop when I asked him if he could let me have a list of any adjustments that he wanted made to the car. "That won't be necessary," he said brightly, borrowing a pair of overalls from one of the mechanics and diving under the bonnet. "I am quite happy to do them myself."

Following the RAC, I decided to visit the Dubai Rally as a spectator, partly to see if there might be a possibility of picking up some private Quattro business there. Although banned in most places, Group B cars were still allowed to compete in the Middle East Championship, so I thought there might well be some interest. It was a trip that later turned out to be very worthwhile indeed – but not quite in the way I had expected.

While there, I bumped into Bill Whiter of Rothmans. I'd first met Bill back in our Rothmans Ford glory days when he was with Rothmans UK. He was now their Middle East Promotions Manager but not for much longer, it emerged. He told me rather sadly that the Dubai Rally was to be the last event for Saeed Al Hajri and his Rothmans Porsche, after which Rothmans would be withdrawing altogether from the Middle East. Naturally, I commiserated with him but didn't think a great deal more about it at the time.

A few weeks later, I was in Spain, taking a short holiday break before the start of the 1988 season, when I got a message from my office to ring Saeed Al Hajri in Qatar as soon as possible. I am always curious when people that I don't know that well suddenly want to talk to me urgently so although, as a rule, I try not to get involved in business when I'm on holiday, I decided to give him a call.

He immediately asked if there was any way that I would

consider flying back to England to meet him in London the next day as there was something he wanted to talk to me about. And, apart from that, did I happen to have an Audi Quattro available for him to drive in the Qatar Rally?

In answer to these questions I told him bluntly that I would only interrupt my holiday if he had some really serious business to discuss and that, yes, as a matter of fact I did have a very good A2 Quattro in the workshop. It had been lying there unused since Mohammmed Bin Sulayem drove it in the previous year's Qatar event.

Al Hajri assured me that my journey back to England would not be wasted, so I duly booked a flight out of Malaga for the next morning and sat in my office to await his arrival. He had mentioned during our telephone conversation that he would be bringing his sponsor with him to the meeting to convince me of just how serious he was, but, even so, I could hardly believe my own eyes when he walked in with none other than Bill Whiter! Bill explained that Rothmans had had a rethink about their earlier decision to withdraw altogether from the Middle East and had now resolved to carry on, albeit at a much lower level. They wanted me to provide and prepare the cars.

The deal they were offering was not particularly advantageous in purely financial terms, but it would provide me with two very important opportunities. Firstly, it would enable us to gain a foothold in the Middle East with the Quattro and, secondly, it would provide a valuable secondary source of income for us if the Audi Sport UK Programme were to run into difficulty for any reason. We shook hands there and then and the Quattro was hurriedly repainted in Rothmans colours before being flown to Doha, along with a team of mechanics and a supply of spare parts. The result was a fine 2nd place overall.

Back home, our British Championship campaign with the Audi 200 got off to an absolutely disastrous start when we had to retire from the opening event, the National Breakdown Rally, after a highly embarrassing own goal.

The package negotiated with Audi involved the loan of two fully equipped Audi Sport Germany service vans, along with a sale-or-return arrangement for the spares and equipment that came with them. David Llewellin was again the driver and he was actually in the lead when a farcical error ended his participation. In the middle of the night, at one of the service points, a new and inexperienced mechanic picked up a can of what he thought was petrol and promptly deposited twenty litres of water into the fuel tank!

I suspect that the young man in question never did learn to speak German but I bet he never forgot thereafter that 'Wasser' is German for water, not petrol.

Apart from the loan of the German service vans, that year's package was unusual in that it stipulated that one of the conditions of receiving Factory support was that we should undertake two World Championship events as well as a full British Championship programme. We chose the Portuguese Rally and the Lombard RAC.

The Audi 200 was a large, heavy and rather cumbersome car, nicknamed "The Gentleman's Express" by the Press, but it can't have been that bad because Hannu Mikkola had won the Safari Rally with it the year before and it had also come 3rd in both the Monte Carlo and the Acropolis. We arrived in Portugal in confident mood, hoping that the rough roads might suit such a big, strong car and David was indeed going very well in 6th place when a steering component broke, putting him out.

The Factory insisted that the offending part be air freighted back to Ingolstadt immediately for analysis, but then, mysteriously, a veil of secrecy descended. When I requested a report some days later, I was met by absolute silence, the Factory steadfastly refusing to discuss the reason for the failure despite repeated requests over the next few weeks. Later, I was to wonder whether this signalled the beginning of the end of my relationship with Audi.

At the time we shrugged it off and returned to the Middle East with high expectations of victory in Kuwait, only to be frustrated by disappointment of a very different kind. A relatively short event, it contained fourteen special stages and Saeed Al Hajri was fastest on eleven of them. We therefore won the rally very convincingly indeed but were disqualified about half an hour after the finish following what I consider to have been a very cynical protest from Toyota.

The allegation was that Saeed's co-driver, Steve Bond, had asked for a time card to be altered. Normally, this is indeed a cardinal sin, but in this instance it was perfectly legitimate because the local official at the control point had made a genuine mistake, which he acknowledged on the spot. But because this official had wandered off by the time the protest was lodged and could not be traced, the organisers would not accept that the alteration was fair and relegated us to 2nd place, behind Toyota's Mohammed Bin Sulayem.

I was thoroughly disgusted by the ruthless tactics of the Toyota Middle East Team, who, in all honesty, must have known perfectly well that we were fair and worthy winners. In fact, the alleged infringement happened after Bin Sulayem had passed through this particular time control and was already in the special stage. The alteration to the time card was spotted by one of his friends, who happened to be standing at the control when our car came through. He reported this to Bin Sulayem just before the results became final and he, in turn, promptly instructed his Team manager to protest. I was very, very angry and from then on I kept a very close eye on Toyota who, it may be recalled, were later found guilty of a serious breach of the regulations in the World Championship, from which they were subsequently banned for an entire season.

It has to be said that the Middle East Championship was not for wimps. The competition, particularly between ourselves and Toyota, was ferocious, with no holds barred and all sorts of shenanigans going on. Occasionally it got completely out of control, as when supporters of the rival teams took to throwing rocks onto the road in front of the opposition. At other times it became almost farcical. And although we were completely innocent in Kuwait there was at least one occasion, I must confess, when we gave almost as good as we got.

This was during the 1988 Jordan Rally. We had bought some Avgas aviation fuel from a military airfield – regular procedure on long distance rallies in countries where the regular petrol is very low octane stuff – but on this occasion it had been put into second-hand jerry cans that were full of sediment, which then blocked the filters on the Audi, causing all sorts of problems at a time when we were well ahead.

Chase cars – fast emergency service vehicles – were still allowed at that time and David Nicholson, in a hired Volvo 360, effectively pushed the Audi for about 50 kilometres during one stage, thumping it up the backside every time the engine started pinking and lost power. At one point, the Toyota management team, their suspicions obviously alerted, raced up alongside on the open road and started taking photographs, but this happened on a long downhill stretch where the Audi was just about able to keep going under its own power and after a while they got bored and drove on. We then continued to play bumper cars and just about made it to the next service point.

The filters were changed here, but as we found when we tried to negotiate the last few hundred yards to the time control, the fuel lines were still blocked and the car was stuttering badly. Again, David, in the Volvo, gave it a solid shunt from behind and as the Audi limped up the slope the huge crowd that had gathered then spontaneously took over and pushed it the last few yards up onto the ramp. Nevertheless, the problem was enough to relegate us to 3rd place.

Meanwhile, we had received an insider tip-off from within the Toyota camp that the gearbox in Mohammed Bin Sulayem's car had been modified to the point where it no longer conformed to the homologation papers. Our formal protest was then rejected by the scrutineer on the grounds that we had not been specific enough about the exact nature of the modification, although we suspected that this was a political decision prompted by the organisers' reluctance to see local Arab hero Bin Sulayem kicked out of the rally. This made the disqualification they secured against us in Kuwait even more galling.

In the British Championship, away from all this skulduggery, things were going from bad to worse. On the Welsh Rally, David Llewellin rolled the car whilst in the lead – the third time in a British Championship event that he had contrived to have a spectacular accident right in front of the television cameras, ensuring that the moment would be captured for posterity. Our rotten luck continued on the Scottish, a month later, when electrical problems caused the big car to stop in the middle of a special stage. We did manage to get it started again and eventually nursed it home in 10th position – the only time that year that we actually managed to finish a rally!

A few hours after the Scottish we left for the Jordan Rally, unfortunately taking our electrical problems with us. We led from the start right up until the very last minute when, at the holding control just before the finish, the Quattro, for no apparent reason, simply refused to start. This relegated Al Hajri to 3rd place when another outright victory should have been his.

Given our run of disappointing performances in the British Championship, it came as no great surprise when, soon after returning from Jordan, I received the familiar thank-you-and-goodbye letter from V.A.G (UK) Ltd. They felt that the poor results with the big Audi 200 – not to say the complete lack of results! – were damaging their image and this time there were to be no second thoughts. On Friday, July 1st, 1988 Audi Sport UK was formally disbanded and my seven-year relationship with Audi finally came to an end.

It was very sad to see everything fizzle out in such an anti-climactic way. We had, after all, won seventeen rallies with Audi at a time when they were constantly pushing forward at the very cutting edge of development during that incredibly exciting Group B era. I suppose that my greatest claim to fame will always be the winning of the World Championship with the Rothmans Ford in 1981, but I look back with just as much pride on our record with Audi. It's just a pity that we couldn't have gone out on more of a high.

In fact, the ending of the Audi partnership had consequences for me that went far beyond the loss of their rally business, prompting me to sell the Audi Volkswagen dealership that I had opened with such a flourish and with such high hopes just two years before. With the wisdom of hindsight, the decision to sell was a mistake. It was made partly out of pique, the feeling that if they didn't want me to rally their cars then I didn't particularly want to sell them.

At the same time, I have to admit that the business had not been doing particularly well and I flatter myself that this was largely because I had been so involved in the rallying side that I had had not given the dealership the close personal attention it needed. What with the Audi 200 Programme, the Golf Programme and the Middle East Championship, I had hardly ever been in the office more than two days running.

I have already referred to what I call "the disease" of rallying, that all-consuming addiction to the adrenaline rush of competition that can obsess you to the point where it takes priority over everything else in your life. In that respect, I am the same now as I ever was. Even after all these years of up to seventy-five flights every season, I never tire of the thrill of it all. At the airport, I still go up the stairs two at a time when I'm on my way to a rally. And I never get on the plane thinking: "Oh God, I've got to go to Finland again". Or Kenya, or New Zealand, or wherever the next event happens to be. My enthusiasm has never diminished.

So, with the dealership losing money, with the interests of the staff in mind and with the bank starting to put me under pressure, I jumped at the chance to sell it when the opportunity suddenly arose. The buyers were another local motor group. I knew the CEO of the group quite well because he ran an Audi Quattro that we supplied, and he just happened to mention one day that he would quite like to add an Audi Volkswagen dealership to his group. Almost on the spur of the moment, I told him: "Well, you can have this one if you like." It must have been one of the fastest deals on record, pretty much done and dusted within 24 hours of that first hint of interest.

Freed of that responsibility, and having moved David Sutton Motorsport into a secondary site at Welton, just outside Daventry, which we had been using as a workshop and storage depot and which was not included in the sale, I threw myself into developing the Middle East business with renewed energy.

We were back to being a completely independent private Team and in some ways that was quite refreshing, despite the fact that with no Factory support and no oil or tyre contract, we were having to pay all our own bills. At least we didn't have all our eggs in one basket.

As well as the Rothmans programme with Al Hajri, we had some Audis of our own, including two Coupes that we now entered on the Cyprus Rally, driven by David Llewellin and local champion Vahan Terzian, who was sadly to die in a road accident some years later. Although not as successful as on our previous visit, we did reasonably well.

Meanwhile, I had been to see my old friend Peter Ashcroft at Ford, Boreham from whom I purchased a Works Sierra Cosworth. The price was £37,002.23, a figure I remember very precisely because Mark Deans, the gentleman with whom I completed the formalities of the sale, insisted that I make the cheque out for that exact amount. He wouldn't knock off the £2.23, even for old time's sake!

We decided to debut the car on the Lebanon Rally, an all-tarmac event to which we thought it would be particularly well suited. The only difficulty here was that hostilities were still taking place, although on a much reduced scale, and so it remained, officially, a war zone. This meant that the mechanics we took out had to go on a voluntary basis, since anybody working in war zones automatically forfeited their right to mortgage protection benefits and there were one or two with family commitments who, quite understandably, felt they couldn't take the risk.

The airport was still closed at this time and the only access was by ferry, from Cyprus, but once we got there we received a very warm welcome and were treated like royalty by the organisers, who were keen to signal the beginnings of a return to normality in their beautiful but war-ravaged country.

There were, nevertheless, some uniquely unnerving moments. Al Hajri had taken the precaution of engaging a colourful local character called Andre as a Mr Fixit-cum-chauffeur-cum-minder. A former government official, Andre was definitely the sort of chap you need to have around in these situations and he looked after us very well indeed.

The first slightly alarming sign that things were going to be a little different on this event came when, before driving us out to inspect the course in our heavily liveried Granada estate car, he slipped a 9mm automatic pistol into the glove compartment and handed David Nicholson an AK 47 assault rifle with an instruction to sit with it in his lap.

There were groups of soldiers all over the place in a variety of uniforms, none of which I recognised, and I felt extremely nervous every time we came across one of these groups, never sure whether they were going to smile and wave or open fire.

At one stage we drove up into the mountains of the Bekaa Valley, where we had set up a service point in a bombed out village. As we stood around, the mechanics started encouraging Andre to let off a few rounds and, taking the AK 47 from David, he casually fired a burst at the ruins of a deserted house, which promptly collapsed! I couldn't help wondering, with a shudder, what sort of damage would be inflicted on a human body if you could knock a wall down with one short volley.

The rally itself went really well, Al Hajri managing a brilliant 2nd place overall, a mere 51 seconds behind the eventual winner. Had he not left the road for a full minute early on we might well have had a sensational debut victory. Even so, it marked the start of a process that was to end with the renewal of our relationship with Rothmans and Ford.

Afterwards, Andre escorted us to Junieh to catch the ferry back to Cyprus and as we said our goodbyes he handed me the AK 47 saying: "Here's a little memento of your visit." I declined as politely as possible with the excuse that I felt I might have a little difficulty getting it through the airport security check when I eventually flew back!

One way and another it was a memorable event in a spectacular setting based around Beirut, a city once rightly renowned as the Paris of the Middle East, and I am pleased to see that it is now being considered for inclusion in the World Championship.

SADDAM HUSSEIN: HIS PART IN MY DOWNFALL

Timing is everything. That is as true of life in general as it is of any sport and in Detroit, in November 1988, I managed to get my timing absolutely spot on for once. As our bad luck with the Rothmans Quattro in the Middle East continued with another frustrating retirement for Saeed Al Hajri while in the lead in Oman, I suggested to Rothmans that a move back to Ford might not be a bad idea. We knew for certain that Audi did not have a new car on the drawing board – or anything else that was even remotely competitive – whereas Ford had a lot to offer. And by now I was back in contact with Boreham.

In particular, I had been making overtures to Peter Ashcroft, trying to convince him that David Llewellin was the best British driver around at the time. I actually managed to talk him into lending us a Works car for David to drive in the RAC, but, unfortunately, David then left the road in the snow while well placed and thereafter Peter could not be persuaded that he was still the man to watch.

He was much more receptive, however, to the idea of a renewed tie-up with Rothmans and ourselves in the Middle East, but pointed out that Ford's activities in that region were run from their American headquarters in Detroit. Bill Whiter and I were immediately despatched to the US by Rothmans to open negotiations.

We arrived laden down with film, photographs, magazine articles and every other bit of presentational material we could muster, anticipating that we were going to have our work cut out trying to explain about rallying in the Middle East and convincing them that Al Hajri was not the name of a small village on the outskirts of Doha.

To our amazement, however, it turned out that Ford had

already done their homework very thoroughly indeed and actually knew much more about the Middle East rallying scene that we had ever suspected. The reason why our approach was so opportune was that a Ford embargo in the Middle East had only just been lifted and they were in the process of trying to rebuild their dealer network in the region. Meanwhile, they had no publicity machine in place there and in order to set up some sort of promotion campaign they had already been looking to join forces with a major sponsor for any sporting activity they could get involved in, no matter whether it was racing, rallying, football, basketball or tiddlywinks! Our sudden and unexpected arrival on their doorstep was therefore something of a godsend.

Bill and I came away from the meeting with the promise of a substantial cheque, which, to Ford's credit, arrived at the Rothmans offices very promptly. This was my first introduction to Ford America and I must say that their relaxed way of doing business came as a very pleasant surprise.

In the meantime, I had accepted an invitation to send David Llewellin to the Bettega Memorial rallysprint event in Italy. The result was once again rather disappointing, but at least we had been able to demonstrate to the world that we were back with Ford.

As 1988 finally drew to a close, I joined hands to sing 'Auld Lang Syne' with more than the usual gusto, relieved to be able to put a bad year behind me and looking forward impatiently to the promise of a fresh start. And we certainly got off to a flyer when Saeed won the opening Middle East event, the Qatar Rally, in a brand new Sierra Cosworth. Among those watching was Boreham's Bill Meade, my friend and adviser for more than thirty years, who had come out to lend a helping hand.

With things continuing to go well and Al Hajri's reputation spreading fast, Rothmans decided that he had a publicity value outside the Middle East. In this they were undoubtedly influenced by the fact that he had just been presented with a special Gold Medal by the Saudi Arabian government for services to sport, an accolade prompted by the huge amount of good publicity he had already attracted. We therefore entered him for two World Championship events in New Zealand and Australia.

In New Zealand, where the event was being sponsored by Rothmans themselves, he managed a commendable 6th place overall, despite difficult conditions caused by torrential rain and the added disadvantage of being up against mostly four-wheel-drive opposition in a rear wheel drive Sierra Cosworth. Moving on to Australia, he was again well placed until problems with the rear differential forced his retirement.

Encouraged by his impressive form in these events, Rothmans thought the time was right to let him have a serious crack at becoming the first Arab driver ever to win an International Rally outside the Middle East, a long-time objective of theirs. They selected the remote Vida Rally in the Eastern Bloc state of Bulgaria as a likely venue for this specific purpose, only for Saeed to destroy his two cars in quick succession. The practice car hit a tree and burst into flames and the rally car itself, which I had pre-sold to a private client in Italy, was also extensively damaged. It had to be hurriedly rebuilt before it could be delivered to its new owner, who, I hasten to add, was told exactly why it was a little late coming!

As we moved on to Northern Greece for the Halkidikis Rally, our Team and all our equipment was now spread over three continents – parts of it in the Middle East, some in Europe and a fair bit in Australia. We were, nevertheless, quite relaxed. One of the nice things about our appearances Down Under and in Europe was that we were not involved in a point-scoring Championship chase. We were simply trying to gain maximum exposure for our sponsor and, although obviously keen to achieve the best possible result, we were not under the usual heavy pressure. So, even when the Greek Gods were not very kind to us and Saeed had to retire with head gasket failure while lying in a promising 4th place, we were not too despondent.

By the same token, we were over the moon a few weeks later in Ireland when our luck changed and Saeed won the Cork Rally in convincing style, at last scoring that long-awaited first International victory. Our joy, however, was short-lived. Despite their delight at this achievement, Rothmans had reluctantly come to the conclusion that they could no longer participate in the Middle East Championship with a rear-wheel-drive car, acutely aware that we were tending to be outclassed in some events by the four-wheel-drive opposition.

There were one or two anxious moments when it looked as though they might pull out of the Middle East altogether, leaving us once again high and dry, but thanks partly to some concerted pressure from their local managers on the spot, they agreed instead to have a look at alternative ways of maintaining a presence in motorsport in the region.

Although not widely advertised, there was another Middle East Championship that catered exclusively for Raid Rallying four-wheel-drive vehicles and it was this type of predominantly off-road motorsport in which Rothmans were now interested, particularly as it fitted rather well with the rugged brand image they were trying to promote. I suggested that Ford in the United States might still be able to help in some way with such a Programme and, to this end, Bill Whiter and I headed back to Detroit for some exploratory discussions.

Yet again, our timing turned out to be perfect. Much to our surprise, our announcement that we were not going to continue with the Cosworth met with a very positive response. As they explained, although they had been happy to have any kind of Ford representation in the Middle East when we had originally approached them, the Sierra Cosworth was not actually sold there, since only American products were handled by their local Ford importers and distributors. So, from a strictly commercial standpoint, it wasn't the ideal vehicle to promote. Four-wheel-drive off-roaders would suit them much better.

As luck would have it, our visit happened to coincide with the famous off-road Baja 1000 event in Mexico and we were invited to go along as guests of Ford so that we could see exactly what was involved and what they had to offer. We flew to Los Angeles and drove down from there to Ensenada in Mexico, where we spent a few very pleasant and usefully informative days talking to Ford engineers and other off-road experts. Afterwards, flying back overnight from Los Angeles to London, it took Bill and I just two or three hours of planning at 37,000ft to create the Rothmans Ford Desert Racing Team.

I was more than happy to get involved in the relatively unfamiliar world of Raid Rallying. For one thing, no other British Team had experience of this form of rallying, which features long distance events that are a bit like mini-marathons, and I welcomed the opportunity to add another string to my bow. Apart from that, I liked the idea of a fresh challenge and a change of scene.

Our Team was to be based around the Ford Bronco T4, driven by Saeed Al Hajri with Fred Gallagher as his co-driver. I had bumped into Fred at a Toyota celebratory champagne party following the Dubai Rally, in which our Rothmans Sierra had marked its farewell appearance with another retirement. Fred had announced that he would be available once his Toyota contract ended after the first two events of the 1990 season and would be delighted to join us. I thought at the time that it would be a good move because Fred had won the Safari Rally on a number of occasions and I felt that his experience with that sort of event could only enhance the image of the Team. It was a decision that I later came to regret.

As a temporary stand-in for Fred on those first two events I brought in David Nicholson, a capable and experienced navigator who had also been working for us as a co-ordinator, a job he later went on to do for David Richards with the Prodrive Allstars Team.

We made our debut in Dubai and although we only managed 6th place overall, the Bronco made an immediate impact. This was the first time it had competed anywhere outside mainland USA so there was enormous interest from the Press in the Middle East, who dubbed it "the Mean Machine". I should like to add here that it was the American components that failed during that first event, while the British contribution to the engineering and design proved more than adequate.

In Oman, where the event was run on dried-up river beds and very rough desert terrain, the big, bucking Bronco with its twenty-one inches of suspension travel really came into its own and Al Hajri annihilated the opposition, winning by a margin of over twenty-five minutes.

This impressive performance was then repeated in Jordan, where, despite some problems on the first day, Al Hajri was soon winning the event in such convincing style that we were visited at a service point by Prince Feisal, one of King Hussein's sons, the late King himself being a great rally enthusiast who regularly took part in his own hill climb event.

It was as we were packing up at the end of the Jordan event that, quite innocently and with what I still consider to have been faultless logic, I made by far the most catastrophic decision of my entire career. The next event was to be in Kuwait and rather than haul all our vehicles and equipment back across Saudi Arabia to our home base in Dubai, I reasoned that it would be hugely cost effective and much more sensible to send most of it direct to the Ford importer in Kuwait where we were to be based.

They duly arrived there on August 2nd, 1990 – a date that may possibly ring a bell in your mind. It is certainly embellished on my memory, because, on August 3rd, our little convoy was followed into Kuwait by Saddam Hussein's invading Iraqi army. On this occasion my timing could not have been worse. As a very visible symbol of the hated USA, the local Ford dealership was a prime target and our vans and trucks, together with all their contents, were soon reduced to smouldering, blackened ruins. Altogether, around £350,000-worth of gear went up in smoke – and because the loss had resulted from an act of war, it was uninsured.

Apart from the fact that none of the Team had been hurt, the only other consolation was that the Bronco itself had escaped unscathed, having been left behind in Jordan while Al Hajri's cousin Mubharak, who had been due to drive it to Kuwait along with the rest of the gear, decided to delay his departure while he went off to Cairo with Saeed for a few days rest and relaxation.

David Nicholson and Mubharak went back later to Amman to retrieve it and, with the port of Al Aqabah still under blockade, had no option but to drive it the 1,300 miles across Saudi Arabia to Qatar. This they eventually managed to do, but not without further drama when they were arrested by Jordanian soldiers at the three-way border checkpoint between Jordan, Iraq and Saudi Arabia.

Things had been going fine until Mubharak was spotted trying to sneak a photograph of refugees from Iraq being packed into an articulated lorry in such numbers that they were forced to stand on each other's shoulders. Having met Kate Adie and the BBC news team while he was in Jordan, David, in particular, was aware of just how interested the media would be in such a picture.

David knew that it was risky but Mubharak insisted that nobody would notice if he leaned forward against the windscreen with the camera hidden under his arm. Needless to say, one of the soldiers looked up just as he was clicking the shutter and the Bronco was immediately surrounded. David and Mubharak were then escorted to an army camp deep in the desert where they spent an anxious day in the guardhouse before eventually being released with a severe warning.

The rest of the journey, along a highway crowded with military convoys, was exhausting and nerve-wracking but otherwise uneventful and, after three days' of non-stop driving they eventually arrived in Qatar and deposited the Bronco with the local Ford dealer in Al Hajri's home town of Doha.

The invasion of Kuwait and the Gulf War that followed it were to have disastrous and far-reaching consequences for me. In the longer term, the losses incurred in Kuwait undermined the financial foundations of David Sutton Motorsport in a way that was to lead to the eventual collapse of the entire company. The more immediate problem was that motorsport in the Middle East generally had been cancelled.

In order to keep Rothmans rallying and Al Hajri busy, we hurriedly arranged entries for one or two conventional events in Europe, using a four-wheel-drive Sierra Cosworth. On the Halkidikis Rally, Al Hajri was going well in 3rd place until the front differential exploded on the second day. From Greece we were due to move on to the Cyprus Rally, an event that, as I mentioned earlier, was sponsored by Rothmans, who had always enjoyed a very large market share in that country.

By this time, however, the crisis in the Gulf was escalating fast in the build-up to Desert Storm and the whole of the Rothmans Middle East organisation was in chaos as they closed down their offices all over the region and evacuated staff and their families to safety. This operation was said to be costing them £1 million-a-day in hotel accommodation and, understandably, the future of their rally programme was not high on their list of priorities.

Again, it was no great surprise when I received the familiar "thank you and goodbye" letter. However, with thousands of pounds worth of vehicles and equipment scattered around in Qatar, Dubai and Cyprus, as well as England, this was devastating news for a company already reeling from the financial effects of the Kuwait disaster.

We won a temporary reprieve after it was announced that the Qatar and Dubai Raids would be going ahead as normal despite the political situation and I managed to persuade Rothmans that with Al Hajri still well placed to win the Championship, they should not give up just yet. To my great relief we duly went on to win in Qatar and although engine failure in Dubai forced the Bronco's first-ever retirement, Al Hajri was neverthess crowned

Middle East Desert Raid Champion for 1990.

Given the continuing uncertainty in the Gulf, I was quite pleasantly surprised when both Rothmans and Ford decided to continue with the Bronco Programme the following year. This was with the proviso that Ford would like the Team to make one appearance in America. We chose the Nissan 400 event in Las Vegas, which I felt would provide some much needed light relief. As I mentioned before, it is very nice every now and again to enjoy the luxury of competing in a well-organised event in an attractive environment without having to worry about scoring Championship points – but in this instance we got a bit more than I'd bargained for.

The format for the Nissan 400 is unusual, to say the least. It involves four laps of a 100-mile circuit through the desert and at the end of each lap you enter a stadium for a sort of Super Special Stage, complete with artificial jumps and water splashes. The event is also open to every conceivable type of vehicle including motorcycles with sidecars, trikes, quad bikes and small trucks, all mixed in together and starting at ten-second intervals.

During a previous visit, I had been taken up in a helicopter by the organisers for a bird's eye view and had been surprised by how slow the pace seemed to be. I confidently told our Team: "We can't fail to win this." Just how wrong I was about that became clear as soon as Saeed and David Nicholson got out on the course. It was only then that they came to realise that there was a very good reason why everybody was going so slowly, namely the extreme severity of the terrain over which they had to drive.

It turned out to be a massive test of stamina and endurance that left Al Hajri so exhausted at the end that he had to be lifted out of the cab, still in the sitting position, and taken back to his hotel to be checked over by a doctor.

The drivers got bounced around so much that many of them had taken the precaution of fitting special suspension seats with sheepskin covers to prevent saddle sores, along with wire mesh windows to keep them cool in the heat of the Nevada Desert.

Many of the cars had a three-man crew, taking it in turns to drive, but the eventual winner was a character known as 'Iron Man' Ivan Stewart, who drove alone in a modified Toyota pick-up with a central steering wheel and a special tube that allowed him to relieve himself while still on the move! With no such refinements, Al Hajri did well to manage 4th in class, covering the 400-mile course in just over nine-and-a-half hours.

One way and another, it wasn't a very happy event for poor Saeed, who had earlier suffered another rather nasty shock when I chartered a light aircraft and took him on a sightseeing trip over and around the Grand Canyon. This was truly spectacular and I would recommend the experience to anyone. The only problem on this occasion was that we ran into a pocket of quite severe air turbulence at one point and as the little plane was hurled about the sky, Saeed turned to me with a look of terror. At that moment I learned that it is possible for even a deeply suntanned Arab to turn a whiter shade of pale!

After Las Vegas it should have been back to serious business with the Tunisian Raid, but this was cancelled at the last minute because of the Gulf War and so our next competitive event became instead the Cuenca Raid in Spain. As Rothmans had finally made up their minds that there would be no conventional rallying that season, the entire Sierra Cosworth Team had been sold to BP in Turkey, who later went on to enjoy considerable success with this equipment. So, to make up for the cancellations in the Middle East we had decided instead to enter the Bronco in some European Raid events.

For the Cuenca Raid an extra member joined the Team. I had been asked by Rothmans if I could suggest a freelance motorsport journalist who could be hired to follow the Team and issue pre-event, on-event and post-event stories. As it happened, I had bumped into John Foden in a bar in Bath some weeks earlier and he had mentioned in passing that John Davenport was not as busy as he would like to be and was desperately seeking work. I had known John for many years and had no hesitation in recommending his journalistic skills to Rothmans, but this was another decision I was to regret later.

I was much more upset at the time about the manner in which defeat was snatched from the jaws of victory in the event itself, thanks entirely to the laziness of the driver and co-driver. We were well in the lead when the engine stalled shortly after the Bronco had forded a river. Unbelievably, the crew just sat there, churning away on the starter until the battery failed and we were forced to retire. When I arrived on the scene with a mechanic, he simply removed the air cleaner, drained the water and re-started the engine within a minute! It should have been an easy victory and the guilty parties received very strongly worded letters from both myself and Rothmans as a result of their extraordinary lapse of concentration.

The next event on the schedule was the Sardinian Raid. This actually starts on mainland Italy before moving on to the rocky little island with its notoriously narrow roads. Here, Al Hajri was back to his best, turning in a devastating performance. Fastest over several sections, he would almost certainly have achieved 2nd or 3rd place if only the Bronco had behaved better and could have fitted onto the track more easily.

We had exactly the same problem a few weeks later on the Natoye Raid in Belgium where, once again, Saeed clearly had the fastest car but was unable to make full use of this advantage on the narrow roads. Even so, he still managed to finish 2nd overall.

Although these European outings helped to keep us ticking over, the Rothmans Team was still funded entirely by its Middle East Division so it was there that we had to make our presence felt. In October 1991, the situation in the Gulf having eased, we returned for the Dubai Raid in reasonably confident mood and were actually in the lead when the engine suddenly blew up.

For Rothmans, this proved to be the last straw and shortly

afterwards they formally ended a relationship that had been hanging in the balance ever since the start of the Middle East crisis. Despite this, it came as a terrible blow that knocked us sideways. I was upset because I felt that our results for the year had not been too bad, considering the special problems that we had faced. It was doubly frustrating because a smaller version of the Bronco, known as the Explorer, had already arrived from the States and I had been very confident that this would give us a real edge the following year.

I was also bitter about the particular circumstances in which Rothmans had finally been prompted to call it a day. For most of the year we had been trying very hard to find a way of extracting more power from the Bronco to compensate for its heavy two-ton weight. Through Ford in America I eventually managed to acquire some special cylinder heads, plus a different block and crankshaft and, on the recommendation of John Davenport, I entrusted the work of modification to an engine builder he had used during his days at Austin Rover.

When the Bronco was flown back from Dubai to be prepared for the next event, it didn't take us long to discover clear evidence that the reason for the catastrophic failure of the new engine was negligence on the part of the people who had rebuilt it for us. I maintain to this day that if John Davenport had taken a more sympathetic attitude and had spoken up on our behalf to Rothmans in this respect, then possibly they might have taken a different view.

As it was, I suddenly found myself once again facing a crisis, with only one small secondary programme to keep us going, and even that not guaranteed to continue beyond the end of the season. It had come about earlier that year following an approach from an Arab driver called Mamdouh Khayat. A Saudi Arabian of considerable education but not a huge amount of talent as a driver, Khayat had come to us with a ready-made and apparently gilt-edged sponsor in the shape of SAMAREC – the Saudi Arabian Manufacturing and Refining Corporation.

This was the outfit that owned and ran all the country's oil interests and it had decided to promote a selection of the country's leading sportsmen. The only oddity was that it should have included a rally driver among the beneficiaries, given that motorsport of any kind was banned in Saudi Arabia at the time! This was apparently because a section of the Koran could be interpreted in such a way as to suggest that motorsport was not in keeping with its teaching.

As far as we were concerned there had been plenty of good reasons to get involved with Khayat. For one thing, the programme of events that he had in mind – the Halkidikis, Cyprus, Lebanon and Algarve Rallies – dovetailed very neatly with our existing Rothmans programme. What's more, all these were very pleasant events in the sunshine, without the pressure of having to chase Championship points. And apart from giving us a useful second string to our bow, it also provided us with an opportunity to return to conventional rallying.

We soon enabled Khayat to rack up a couple of notable firsts. One of them came before he'd even had a chance to get behind the wheel of the car when I used my contacts to get him issued with Saudi Arabia's first-ever Competition Licence. Disappointingly for him, he had to be officially registered as No 2 since the government insisted on holding back No 1 in case it might be required for a special celebrity. He then went straight out and secured 9th place in the Halkidikis Rally, thereby becoming the first Saudi to score a point in a European Championship event. Not a bad start to his International career!

He should have done even better in Cyprus, where he was heading for an almost unbelievable 2nd place until he got carried away and crashed. He made up for this mistake in Lebanon, where he did indeed finish 2nd, but blotted his copybook badly again in Portugal, destroying both the practice car and the rally car itself within the space of a few hours. He demolished the rally car the day before the event, while filming a preview item for the Saudi Arabian television crew that followed us everywhere. The mechanics worked all night to rebuild the practice car so that he could still start the rally, only for him to wreck that, too, after just four or five stages.

In spite of these incidents I remained intensely loyal to him, to his sponsor and to his family. However, I am sad to say that this loyalty was not returned when, during the following year, I faced my greatest hour of need.

DOWN AND OUT

As soon as I received the news that the Rothmans Ford Team was to be disbanded I left immediately for Saudi Arabia, anxious now to confirm the deal with Mamdouh Khayat for the 1992 season. I went out armed with a visa document that Khayat assured me would be acceptable, but this turned out not to be the case and I spent sixteen anxious and frustrating hours marooned in the transit lounge at Jeddah airport while he and his friends in the government tried in vain to get me into the country. Thankfully, the journey was not entirely wasted because I did eventually manage to come away with a signed contract.

Khayat's main objective was to win the Middle East Championship. This was not beyond the realms of possibility because both Saeed Al Hajri and Bin Sulayem had set their sights on the World Championship, Bin Sulayem with Marlboro in a Toyota while Al Hajri was still with his long-time friends at Rothmans, but this time in a Mitsubishi.

With his main rivals safely out of the way, a fast-improving Khayat would definitely have a chance, as he proved in the opening event in Qatar, where he drove our 4x4 Sierra Cosworth to an excellent 2nd place. If he could maintain that sort of form with some careful driving, then he might indeed go on to fulfil his ambition of becoming the first Saudi driver to take the title.

Meanwhile, during a visit to the Racing Car Show, I had come across Steve Bagnall, my old sparring partner from Audi Sport UK, who showed me his latest offering, the Volkswagen Polo G40 racing car. With everything going so quiet on the rallying scene – a disturbing trend reflected in the fact that the Scottish Rally of 1991 featured only fifty-five cars in a field that included fourteen military Land Rovers – I was ready to consider anything that would keep me busy and after some discussion, plus the promise of further support from Shell, I agreed to buy one of these cars and race it throughout 1992, with my old and trusted friend, David Llewellin, as driver.

With nine Top Ten finishes in ten races, this one-make programme was to provide some of the very few bright spots in what was otherwise to be a traumatic year for me. Apart from anything else, it was a great pleasure to be working with David again. At the same time, I welcomed the opportunity to keep a foot in the Audi Volkswagen door.

By the spring of 1992, David Sutton Motorsport Ltd was starting to get into serious financial difficulty. The combination of the losses in Kuwait, the devastating effects of the Gulf War on our Middle East Programmes and the ending of the Rothmans contract, together with the general economic recession in the UK, was threatening to overwhelm us. Short of money and overstocked with unwanted and obsolete competition vehicles that we couldn't sell, including rear-wheel-drive Sierra Cosworths and Ford Broncos, we were pretty much living hand-to-mouth on the income from Mamdouh Khayat's Saudi contract.

As we waited anxiously for each new instalment of money to come through, things were often very tight. There was one particular occasion when, with the Algarve Rally coming up, we badly needed a fair amount of petty cash to take with us at a time when we were already on the very limit of our overdraft. In desperation, I rang a colleague who, I suspected, might well have experienced the same sort of problem at various times and asked him whether he had any ideas about how to get around it. Without a moment's hesitation he advised: "Bash the plastic!"

I don't know why I hadn't thought of that myself. Especially during the time when Jill and I had kept a house in America, we had been showered with credit cards, most of which were still lying around, unused. So, one afternoon, the two of us just walked up and down Daventry High Street, punching these cards into different machines, and within a very short space of time we had successfully extracted several thousand pounds out of various holes in the wall. I remember this episode particularly well because for a long time afterwards we could only afford the minimum monthly repayments and it was to be ten years before I finally paid off the last one.

By early May, 1992, we had again reached a cash-flow crisis point where, in order to fulfil the terms of the Saudi contract, we needed to borrow extra money to fund the Jordan Rally and to tide us over until the next contract payment was due, immediately after the event. To this day, I still cannot quite believe that when I asked the bank for a short-term loan of £25,000, to be repaid as soon as the payment from the Saudi government agency came through eighteen days later, they refused to sanction it.

At the time of my request, David Sutton Motorsport Ltd's current account was actually in credit, its existing business loan account was ahead of its payment schedule and it had assets officially estimated to be worth £550,000. And, while one or two of our creditors were indeed starting to write fairly nasty letters, the company had not received any writs, winding up orders or other serious threats. All this, plus the fact that I had been a "valued customer" of Lloyds Bank for thirty-six years, apparently counted for nothing. When I mentioned this the reply was: "We are now in the money business, not the people business." There was no sign of the best china coming out now as I was bluntly informed that further credit would not be forthcoming.

By this time, the mechanics had already arrived in Jordan from the previous event in Lebanon, while David Nicholson, along with my stepson, Guy, who was working for us at this time, were bringing the car and the support vehicles from the Eastern Mediterranean, down though Syria and into Jordan. Back in England, meanwhile, I was starting to panic as I dealt with an increasing barrage of angry phone calls and final demands from people asking why their bills had not been paid.

Among Jill's close friends at this time was a lady lawyer with whom she shared an interest in horses. Occasionally, when the two of them had been out riding together, I would meet up with them in the village pub afterwards for a drink and one evening, at the end of a particularly bad day in the office, I started pouring out my troubles. After listening very sympathetically, this lady went away and wrote me a long letter of friendly advice, the bottom line of which was that if one were knowingly to operate a company that was technically insolvent, then the directors risked going to jail.

That letter frightened the life out of me. There was no way, at the age of 52, that I fancied a spell in the Grey Bar Motel as a guest of Her Majesty! I talked all the options through with Jill and after a great deal of agonising we reluctantly came to the conclusion that the best course of action would be to go into voluntary Administrative Receivership. And so it was that on the afternoon of May 14th, 1992, I went to the bank's offices in Colmore Row, Birmingham and effectively signed the company away.

I would like to stress that at this stage we had not gone bust, we had not been declared bankrupt and we were not forced into Receivership. By going into Voluntary Administrative Receivership we had simply handed the day-to-day running of the company over to the bank. The irony of this situation was that the bank effectively ended up giving the Receiver the money to run the company that it had refused to give to me.

Looking back now, I wish that I hadn't given in so easily, because I think that if I'd held on for just a little bit longer I might have been able to weather the storm. At the time, however, I was petrified by the mere thought of going to prison and I wanted to be seen to be doing everything by the book. As further evidence of this, I should mention that on the day before I formally offered the company for Receivership I sold a rally car for £25,000 and was paid in cash. Everybody I have ever spoken to about this since then has told me that I should have put the money in my back pocket to help keep Jill and I afloat for the next couple of years, instead of which I declared it and handed it over to the bank to reduce the company liabilities.

It took about two hours to go through all the formalities with the bank that afternoon – two of the most depressing hours of my life. But that was by no means the final act of the drama. As the meeting broke up and I left the bank's offices, it turned out that, quite by coincidence, Receiver Hedley Brunt and I had parked our cars in the same street and we found ourselves walking together to retrieve them. I say 'our' cars but I was actually driving Jill's estate car since I no longer had the authority to drive my company car. Anyway, as we walked along we fell into a conversation during which Mr. Brunt asked: "Were you serious when you said just now that if we were to go ahead with the Jordan Rally next week we would receive £20,000 from the Saudi sponsors a few days later?"

"Of course," I replied. "If we fulfil the terms of the contract there is no reason to suppose that Mamdouh Khayat and his Saudi sponsors will not pay us the money that falls due at the end of this month. And up until now they have always paid up right on time." I also reminded him that Khayat, co-driver David Nicholson and the rest of the Team were already in position in Jordan so that all we needed to do to fulfil our part of the contract was to pay for a few airline tickets and hotel rooms.

"In that case, we will do the rally," he said decisively. "And it would obviously make sense for you to be out there in your usual capacity to make sure everything runs smoothly."

A few days later I flew out to Amman, accompanied by a 'minder' in the shape of the Receiver's manager, Nigel Spearing, a gentleman who was destined to prove less than totally helpful, as far as I was concerned, in what was clearly an awkward situation.

As soon as we arrived in Jordan I immediately convened a meeting at which I informed the drivers and mechanics and everyone else concerned with the Team that David Sutton Motorsport Ltd was no longer under my control and that I was present purely in my role as Team Manager. I then introduced Mr Spearing, who assured all the mechanics that apart from the fact that they were now working for him and his Receiver rather than me, it would otherwise be business as usual.

This was not quite the case, as my loyal mechanics were only to find out much later when Spearing reneged on this understanding and announced that they would be paid only from the date of the appointment of the Receiver and not for the previous weeks during which they had already been in Jordan, preparing for the event. As far as that period was concerned, they would be regarded as unsecured creditors.

I was very angry about this because the mechanics, had they known at the time that this was going to be the case, would have been in a position to negotiate for payment in full on the basis that they might otherwise decide to down tools and go home there and then, leaving the Team high and dry. As it was, Mamdouh Khayat beat them to it.

On the eve of the rally, he called a meeting in his hotel room at which I was not permitted to be present. During this meeting, he was assured by Nigel Spearing of our continuing commitment to the full programme, which we were ready to complete according to the terms of the original contract. On this basis, Khayat agreed to go ahead with the Jordan event and signed a document, witnessed by David Nicholson, stating that a payment of £20,000 would be put through immediately afterwards.

He then went out and drove very well to secure 4th place, raising himself to 2nd in the Championship and momentarily boosting morale all round. I dared to hope at this stage that there was still a chance that the company might be able to survive if only he could keep this up. That hope was soon dashed, however, when the money failed to materialise and Khayat himself suddenly vanished without a word, refusing to respond

The aftermath of the extraordinary crash in Portugal in which our two Escorts both went off the road at exactly the same point, ending up on top of one another.

A much more welcome one-two for the same crews as (l to r) Arne Hertz, David Richards, Ari Vatanen and Hannu Mikkola celebrate after coming 1st and 2nd on the Welsh Rally in 1980.

One of my favourite pictures from one of my favourite rallies (above), with Ari Vatanen and David Richards on their way to victory in the 1981 Acropolis while Meteora provides a spectacular, towering backdrop.

On the Acropolis victory podium (left) with David and Ari and (below) with Hannu Mikkola and Rothmans promotion manager John Newcombe.

The full Rothmans Ford team on parade (above) before the last event of the Championship-winning 1981 season.

Celebrating the moment of victory with Ari Vatanen (left).

(below) Ian Parry, once Jill's co-driver, now with Prodrive, and Ron Lumley (right), my chief mechanic for many years.

Michele Mouton and Fabrizia Po??
in the 1985 Manx Rally (above le??
They destroyed this awesome SI
Quattro a few stages later while
Hannu Mikkola (above right), we??
from last to 1st in the 1982 Scott??
Rally with a stunning exhibition o??
driving.

John Queenborough at Pike's Pea??
(above) and (left)Hannu demon-
strates the power of four-wheel
drive at a Rallysprint in Wales.

Michele Mouton in 1985 (right), the greatest woman rally driver of all time.

The Audi/Volkswagen dealership in Daventry shortly before its official opening by Hannu Mikkola, seen below with Jill and me.

David Llewellin (right) and Phil Short celebrate a rare victory for the relatively under-powered Group A Audi Quattro Coupe in Cyprus in 1987 and (below) Barfields Farm, the home we lost in 1992 thanks partly to Saddam Hussein.

Monte Carlo or bust - a study in concentration as I negotiate an icy Alpine road in the Mk VI Bentley with Ivor Gordon and David Nicholson.

At the finish with Ivor (centre) and David Nicholson (right).

Left: American John Buffum and co-driver Fred Gallagher on the Acropolis and Andrew Wood (below) putting a Group A VW GTi through its paces.

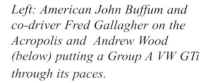

Jill and I with Hannu and Arja Mikkola and baby Juha after Juha's christening in Helsinki.

With Juha and his younger brother Vesa (left), and (below) Hannu and Juha with Hannu's 1995 London-Mexico Escort in which they drove the 2000 London-Sydney marathon.

to our frantic phone calls and faxes.

While we tried desperately, but in vain, to establish exactly what was going on, the Receiver, as a sign of his good faith, authorised all the vehicles to be moved up to Junieh, just north of Beirut, in readiness for the Lebanon Rally. With considerable presence of mind, David Nicholson hid them away in a secret location in the basement car park of a block of flats. Still there was no word from Khayat. Then, after a couple of weeks, he finally came out of hiding to reveal that he had actually been in Italy, secretly negotiating a new deal with an Italian-based Lancia Team to whom he would be transferring both his allegiance and his budget, with immediate effect.

I have to say that this was something he was perfectly entitled to do, since most contracts include a clause that renders them automatically null and void should a company become bankrupt or go into Receivership. But the manner in which he went about it did not seem to me to reflect well on a man whom I had always found to be rather a tricky character, permanently surrounded by a large and less than totally charming entourage of relatives and hangers-on led by his brother, Abdullah.

He actually did very well with his new Team, building on the great start we had given him and going on to achieve his aim of winning the Middle East Championship. The rather intriguing postscript to this, however, is that he then disappeared once again from the rally scene and, as far as I am aware, never drove again, although some time later he did pop up as a commentator on F1 for a Middle East television channel.

His defection and the collapse of the Saudi deal removed the last lingering hope of keeping David Sutton Motorsport Ltd afloat. Two weeks later, Jill and I were officially made redundant and, of the remaining staff, only chief mechanic John O'Connor and my secretary, Pauline Thomas, were kept on to help the Receiver dispose of the vehicles and stock as the company was finally wound up and all its assets went under the hammer. In the end, it was a sorry case of: 'Will the last person to leave the building kindly switch off the lights'.

It is a humbling experience to be politely dismissed from your own office with the words: "I'm afraid you will not be required any more – don't bother to come in next week." I walked away feeling sad, ashamed and not a little angry.

My anger was directed mostly against the banks that were pulling the plug on little companies like mine at the rate of something like 4,000 every month at that particular time. Many of those that went to the wall should not and would not have done so if the banks had been a bit more flexible – instead of which they were so busy propping up high profile failures such as Polly Peck and Robert Maxwell's Pergamon, in which they had so heavily and unwisely invested, that they had no time to worry about the smaller and often more deserving businesses that were being pushed under.

There were other things that also made me very bitter in the aftermath of the collapse. For instance, our annual accounts for the previous year showed that the company had assets worth £550,000 and yet those same assets, once they had been handed over to the Receiver for liquidation, were sold off for a fraction of that amount. The reason for this is that the Receiver's only aim is to get rid of them as quickly as possible once the company has gone into liquidation, but it broke my heart to see valuable cars and equipment going under the hammer and being virtually given away.

I was also very surprised to notice, when draft accounts were produced at the first creditors' meeting, that the Receiver himself had charged a fee of £30,000, despite assuring us beforehand that ours was such a simple and straightforward case that his fee would be no more than about £15,000. When I complained to the bank about this I was told bluntly: "We never challenge Receivers' fees."

Nowadays, I am pleased to say, accountants have to compete for Receivership business with competitive tenders, a change in practice that came about after it was acknowledged that some accountants specialising in this sort of work were making millions out of Receiverships that had not been negotiated in advance.

I have to admit that this was the least of my concerns at the time. Simple survival was what I had to worry about, not just in the material sense but also in terms of self-respect. Apart from the vague stigma that inevitably attaches itself to anyone whose business has failed, there are all the little public humiliations that you have to endure when you have gone from something to nothing, especially when you are living in a small village where everybody knows everybody else's business.

Jill and I had moved to our very attractive corner of Warwickshire when we relocated the business from West London to Daventry. Our first home was a converted windmill at Napton, complete with an indoor swimming pool built into the basement. This all seemed wonderfully romantic until the windmill's sails broke loose from their moorings one night during a violent storm, with the result that the trailing ropes lashed all the tiles off the roof.

Shortly after that, we got the chance to buy Barfields Farm, just outside the nearby village of Stockton. The house itself needed an awful lot doing to it but was in a beautiful location, with bags of potential for development. It also included a considerable acreage of farmland where Jill could keep the horses, which had become her main interest after she retired from rallying, and where I could walk the dogs extensively. We spent the next few years doing it up extensively to create a striking ranch-style home that at the height of the eighties property boom was worth around £450,000. Apart from the horses, from which Jill had started to breed, we had 150 sheep grazing the meadows.

With further houses in Marbella and California, plus a private twin-engine Cessna 340, a Princess 33 motor yacht and a couple of Audi Volkswagen dealerships, we had been seen to be doing very well for ourselves in the years following my World Championship-winning success and this only added to our discomfiture when our circumstances suddenly changed so disastrously – especially when, for a brief period, I was reduced to signing on for the dole.

I felt particularly uncomfortable about doing this, if only out of a sense of pride, but I was persuaded by friends and family that I had every right to take advantage of the system into which I had been paying for thirty years. Their attitude was that I should look at it rather like making a claim on an insurance policy.

Jill and I had sunk every penny we had into David Sutton Motorsport, to the extent that, when things started to go wrong, we had re-mortgaged the farm and had offered it up as security. So, when the crunch came, we were not only unemployed and broke – apart from the small redundancy payment I had received – but didn't even have a home we could call our own. I reluctantly accepted that I would have to swallow my pride and sign on until such time as I could get back on my feet.

I still shudder at the recollection of the morning that I turned up to register with the DHSS in Leamington Spa. I had been told to report at 10.00 am and arrived early to find myself joining the queue of rather depressed-looking individuals that had already formed up, waiting for the doors to open. I felt enormously self-conscious as we shuffled forward, waiting for our turn to be called forward to a cubicle to give our details and to satisfy the authorities that we were actively looking for work. Had I really fallen this far since being feted as a World Championship winner?

I was eventually interviewed by a young girl who asked me what I did for a living and when I explained that I was a motorsport consultant and rally team manager she looked at me rather blankly and said: "We've never had one of those before."

As there was no regular public transport operating between our village and Leamington, I was allowed to collect my dole money from the village post office instead of having to go and queue for it at the DHSS offices each week. Although much more convenient in some ways, this arrangement proved to be even more acutely embarrassing in others, since the post office was at the heart of a small community in which I was a well known and, I like to think, a respected figure. It was actually located almost next door to the local pub and I would try to pick the quietest part of the day to sneak past, praying that I wouldn't bump into too many of the regulars. It was a bizarre feeling.

It is the way in which the mundane, everyday things in your life suddenly change that brings it home to you just how far you have fallen from grace. Another of my more painful memories from this period is of going with Jill to Sainsbury's to do the weekly food shopping and suddenly realising, as we started to fill our trolley in the usual way, that we had better check to make sure we had enough cash to pay for everything. With our credit cards already over the limit, we had to be very careful that we didn't put ourselves in the highly embarrassing situation where we reached the checkout and had to put something back on the shelf.

Something else that you very soon discover in these circumstances is that, just like it says in the words of that old song, nobody wants to know you when you're down and out. After the news that we had gone under hit the front pages of the motorsport Press, only a handful of people in the business bothered to ring me to ask how I was and to offer words of sympathy and moral support.

In the days immediately after being made redundant from my own company I was in a state of shock. It wasn't easy to see any kind of future for myself at first because, although it's relatively easy to recover from a setback like that in your forties, it is very different when you are on the wrong side of fifty and virtually unemployable. I did, however, have one lifeline to grab at. For me it was to be a case of back to the future.

BACK TO THE FUTURE

The driving careers of most amateur rally enthusiasts tend to follow the same pattern, passing through three distinct phases. They start off as young boy racers, getting heavily involved in club events and spending every spare moment and every bit of spare cash on preparing and rallying their cars. They then get married, have kids, swap the rally car for a family saloon and devote all their energy for the next few years to building up their businesses or climbing the executive ladder, with all their money going on mortgages and school fees.

By the time they are 45 or 50, however, with the kids off their hands and the mortgage paid off, they may be lucky enough to find themselves in possession of a little bit of disposable income with which to have fun. And assuming that they have not taken a mistress with expensive tastes or gone through a ruinous divorce – or both! – they then have the choice of the usual big boys' toys such as Ferraris, yachts and helicopters or they can return to their first love - rallying. And if they are sensible enough to choose the latter, they usually want to have a classic car in which to indulge their newly rekindled passion.

Historic rallying really started to take off in an organised way in the late seventies, born out of nostalgia for the Mini Coopers, Austin Healeys, Saabs and Volvos. It got a tremendous boost from the RAC 'Golden Fifty' 50th Anniversary event in 1982 and the revival of the Mille Miglia the following year, by which time the FISA had classified Historic cars and had issued regulations. The first of several RAC Historic Rallies was then run in 1991 and was won by Timo Mäkinen in a Mini Cooper S. What had begun primarily as a social branch of rallying for collectors was becoming increasingly competitive.

In the years immediately prior to the demise of David Sutton

Motorsport I had begun to take a growing interest in the Historic side of rallying, buying up old cars, restoring them and selling them on mainly as a sideline to keep the workshop busy during those occasional quiet periods when there wasn't much happening on the regular rallying front. When one or two clients then asked me carry out bare metal restoration projects on the defunct Group B Audis I decided to form a separate company, Historic Motorsport Ltd, through which to run this side of the business.

At the same time, I myself had been tempted back into competitive driving in a small way. I had always retained a deep nostalgic affection for the rally cars I grew up with, especially the Ford Lotus Cortina, and during a visit to America I happened to stumble across a particularly fine example that had been discovered under an apple tree in an orchard near San Francisco - Southern California being a particularly fruitful source of rust-free historic cars owing to the very dry atmosphere in that part of the world.

A standard model that had been in the same ownership for nearly 20 years, it was offered complete with a full set of spares, including a new bonnet, and I snapped it up with a view to converting it into an exact Works replica. In the meantime, I was impatient to try it out and as soon as it arrived from America I took it on the 1991 Targa Rusticana in Wales pretty much as it was, the first time I had driven a rally car in competition for sixteen years!

The Targa Rusticana is a lot of fun, a real old-fashioned, traditional night thrash, flat out over narrow, bumpy, winding Welsh mountain roads. With David Nicholson as my co-driver, I thoroughly enjoyed every minute but, even so, I was totally flabbergasted when it was announced at the breakfast prizegiving the next morning that we had come 10th overall and 1st in class! This was despite problems with a dynamo that reduced the spotlights to candle power every time the revs dropped and dodgy front suspension that caused them to point straight down at the ground every time the brakes were applied.

David Nicholson also made some fairly caustic comments about my fading eyesight, complaining that although I was "frighteningly" fast when there were steep banks or hedges on either side of the road to give me a line, I didn't seem to know quite where I was once things opened out a bit more! I'm not sure whether it was fear of my driving or the bumpy ride that caused David to throw up as we negotiated a particularly tough and twisty section known as the Devil's Staircase!

At around the same time David and I, along with my best and oldest friend, Ivor Gordon, took part in the Historic Monte Carlo Challenge in a Mk VI Bentley belonging to Ivor, a specialist dealer in classic Rolls Royces and Bentleys and one of the world's leading authorities on the history of these marques. The rally turned out to be a somewhat more dramatic adventure than we had bargained for as atrocious weather conditions in the Alps turned the roads into skating rinks and made life extremely difficult in the unwieldy three-ton Bentley. To add a further element of unpredictability, Ivor had never driven at this level before and was basically learning as we went along!

An early misjudgement within the first couple of hours resulted in a collision with a road sign that put a large V-shaped dent in the bumper and then got wedged under the car in such a way that it effectively jacked up the entire front end. As we battled on through fog, snow and ice we then hit the Armco barrier on a sharp bend and, once again, managed to ramp the car up on top of it, leaving it hanging in mid-air. Fortunately, we came across a big snow blower operating nearby and managed to bribe the driver to come and pull us off.

Finally, as we were going down the Col de Turini, one of the most famous stages of the Monte Carlo Rally, we struck sheet ice and, with a bank on one side and nothing but fresh air on the other, we froze in horror as the heavy car slithered into a triple 360-degree spin at a gentle 10mph, eventually coming to rest with its back end stuck in the bank. Very gingerly, we pushed it free and then made our way down by nudging it along against the bank. You couldn't steer it, you couldn't stop it – it was basically three tons of metal with a mind of its own.

Despite this, we were actually lying 13th out of a field of about 150 towards the end, when a puncture then dropped us down to 33rd. We nevertheless won the Spirit of the Rally award as the most unlikely car to complete the course – although it has to be said that some of our navigation had been creative, to put it mildly!

In keeping with the tradition on these events, we had been required to carry dinner suits, as well as spares, in order to be properly attired for the black tie party at the end. Ivor was like a dog with two tails, so proud of himself that he kept the car on prominent display in his West London showroom for two years afterwards – with the dent left in as a sort of badge of honour.

Encouraged by my successful driving comeback in the Targa Rusticana, I borrowed Jill's old ex-Works Cortina from the garage to which it had been sold and set about turning my California car into an exact copy. This turned out to be a big mistake, the whole idea being based too much on pure nostalgia and emotion, without much thought being given to making it properly competitive.

A completely authentic 1966 car simply could not live with other classics from that period, most of which had been modified, within the regulations, to include such refinements as carbon disc pads and Minilite wheels. This became all too clearly apparent when the Cortina made its debut in the 1991 Autoglass RAC International Historic Rally with my old friend Roger Clark at the wheel.

I had decided that if I was going to make my mark with Historic Motorsport then I would need to secure the services of a big name professional driver and Roger was the obvious choice. Not without his own business problems at the time, he gladly accepted the drive. However, even with his genius – and despite the added bonus of being re-united for the event with his 1972 Lombard RAC Rally-winning co-driver Tony Mason, by this time a BBC Top Gear television personality – he could manage no better than 7th.

This disappointing result was absolutely no reflection of Roger's talent. Given the set-up of the car, he actually did very well to get us into the Top Ten, even though he and Tony had been seeded No 1, purely on the basis of their track record and experience. The problem was that the event was totally geared for the Mini Coopers and with the handbrake on the Cortina located under the dashboard and alongside the steering column, it was virtually impossible to do the sort of handbrake turns that were essential on the special stages and on the various auto tests that involved spinning around pylons. We were, nevertheless, first in Class and also won the Team award as part of a three-car Ecurie Cod Fillet entry.

Ecurie Cod Fillet, for anyone not already familiar with the colourful history of this very exclusive club, was originally founded back in the very early sixties by a group of rally enthusiasts from the Stockport Motor Club, led by Roy Fidler and John Hopwood. Roy ran a very successful fresh fish business, hence the name Ecurie Cod Fillet, a humourous take on the grand continental rally teams of the time.

Over the years it has grown into one of sport's most renowned and best-loved institutions, with an invitation-only membership of around 350 that includes almost everyone who's ever been anyone in rallying in the last forty years, from Sir Stirling Moss, who actually started his career as a rally driver, to today's all-powerful rally supremo, David Richards.

Its regular biennial re-union dinners are eagerly awaited highlights of the rally calendar, characterised by that unique brand of irreverent Northern humour so perfectly exemplified by one member, the late Mike Sutcliffe, who left very explicit instructions for his own funeral that included the request that on his last journey from the church to the crematorium, which took in a section of the M62, he should be clocked at 100mph. A high-speed hearse was duly arranged but, on the day, it could sadly only manage 98mph, nevertheless causing a few double takes from startled motorway drivers as it swept past in the outside lane!

Following our somewhat less spectacular performance in the RAC, we went back into the workshop and brought the Cortina bang up-to-date, sacrificing authenticity in favour of stretching the rules to the limit, just like everybody else. And in preparation for our return to the RAC the next year we insisted on subjecting Roger to two days of concentrated testing at Bruntingthorpe. He complained bitterly that he had never worked so hard in his life after we refused to let him go off to the pub for his usual three-hour lunches and instead had him thrashing up and down from dawn 'til dusk with various combinations of dampers and springs and suspension heights and anti-roll bars until we had the car set up to our entire satisfaction.

This all paid off when, with David Nicholson as his co-driver on this occasion, Roger came in 3rd, just nineteen seconds behind the winner. And I might add that if the organisers had stopped certain Scandinavian competitors from using illegal tyres at the beginning of the event, then victory would almost certainly have been ours.

Also taking part in that event, and making his Historic debut in a Mini Cooper that I had prepared for him, was someone who was about to play an enormously significant part in my future. Ignacio Sunsundegui was a larger-than-life character in every sense. A hugely successful Spanish businessman and entrepreneur, whose wide-ranging interests included everything from hotels to the rolling stock service contract for the Spanish equivalent of British Rail, he was also physically imposing, a six-foot-four-inch gentle giant, with a twinkle in his eye and an easy-going, fun-loving manner that endeared him to everyone he met. He also had an all-consuming passion for rallying and the money to indulge it.

Starting off in his early twenties with a Citroën 2CV in 1960, he had progressed through DKWs and Minis to Alpine Renaults and Porsches, competing almost exclusively in Spain and France. An accomplished amateur driver, he was good enough to have secured 3rd place in the Spanish Championship one year and he made a point of never missing the Monte Carlo Rally.

It was in Spain, where I had always had a number of private clients ever since my Clarke & Simpson days, that I first got to know him slightly. However, it wasn't until the mid-Eighties when he grew rather more ambitious and set his sights on owning a serious Group B car, that he became a customer.

Ignacio decided, around 1984, that he would like to add an Audi Quattro to his already extensive collection of cars and as it was well known that I had access to ex-Works models, he naturally sought my help. Over the next few years he bought several from me, starting with the A2 that we had originally built for Stig Blomqvist and in which Stig had won the 1983 RAC. We later went on to supply him with a Sport Quattro and then, finally, the mighty 600bhp S1 that had been driven by Hannu Mikkola.

Although banned from the World Championship in 1986, Group B cars remained eligible for National Championship events in several countries, including Spain, and it was there that Ignacio rallied his Audis with some success, until, in 1991, he rolled the Sport Quattro down the side of a mountain in a monumental accident that left him with several cracked ribs and shook his confidence.

I was summoned to Spain to assess the full extent of the damage to the car and arrived to find one of the most comprehensive Sport Quattro wrecks that I had ever seen. Over dinner, Ignacio then admitted that he wanted it restored purely as a collectors' item, adding that the accident had persuaded him to give up rallying before he did himself some even more serious damage. In his fifties by this time, he had very reluctantly come to accept that he was a bit too old to compete any more at the highest level.

Given that he was one of my few remaining private customers at a time when David Sutton Motorsport was already feeling the pinch, this was not good news. I explained that I was starting to get more involved in Historic cars and suggested that maybe this could be the way forward for him, too, a perfect opportunity to remain actively involved in the sport without exposing himself to quite the same level of risk. To my great delight he picked up on this with considerable enthusiasm, telling me that he had always had a passion for the Mini Coopers in which he had done much of his early rallying.

By a happy coincidence, it just so happened that a Mini Cooper S previously driven by Timo Mäkinen had been advertised in Autosport that very week. Would Ignacio be interested in buying it, I wondered? He promised to think about it.

I had to get up at the crack of dawn the next morning to fly back to England for an important meeting and it was arranged that one of Ignacio's drivers would pick me up at my hotel at 5.30 am and take me to the airport. On the way, the driver passed on the message that Ignacio had given instructions for the Quattro to be transported to England for repair. "And, by the way, he also wants you to go ahead and buy the Mini you talked about last night," he added.

I breathed a sigh of relief. These two projects, together with the service contracts I had with one or two other Quattro owners, would at least enable me to keep Historic Motorsport ticking over. I duly went out and bought the Mini, converted it to left-hand drive and prepared it in time for the Historic RAC, where Ignacio achieved a reasonable result.

He then went on to do the Circuit of Ireland, this being one of his favourite events along with the Scottish and the Monte Carlo Rallies, but he didn't do so well here, being forced to retire after rolling the Mini and leaving it in need of a new body shell. I had decided that I would do the Circuit as well in the Lotus Cortina and fared much better, coming a respectable 5th.

Win, lose or draw, you always come back from Ireland with a monumental and well-earned hangover, but on this occasion I already had more than my fair share of headaches. David Sutton Motorsport was by now in the final throes of its collapse and a few months later it went into voluntary administration. All I was left with was Historic Motorsport and, with no premises, no staff and virtually no business, this was little more than an empty shell of a company at this stage. However, it remained my only hope of survival.

I hurriedly set up a makeshift workshop in the triple garage at Barfields farm. Technically, the property had been repossessed, having been put up as security for loans taken out on behalf of David Sutton Motorsport, but, thankfully, I managed to persuade the bank and the building society to let Jill and I remain there until such time as a buyer could be found. With the economy still in deep recession and the housing market in a state of collapse, this was to take some months, giving me a brief but welcome respite.

Having used my redundancy money to buy back a few odds and ends of unsold workshop equipment and office furniture from the Receiver, I made a point of being at my desk in my office at the farm at 8.30 am sharp on the Monday immediately after being shown the door at Daventry. I spent the next few weeks on the phone and eventually managed to scrape together enough business to justify bringing back the loyal and long-serving John O'Connor to help me out, along with a second mechanic, Ricky Johnson.

We were not too proud to tackle any job at this stage and apart from looking after our one or two private Audi clients, we also carried out whatever routine repair and servicing work we could conjure up in order to keep ourselves busy. But the key figure in the gradual, Phoenix-like re-emergence of Historic Motorsport from the ashes of David Sutton Motorsport was Ignacio.

As well as committing himself to drive a fairly full programme of Historic events with both the Mini Cooper S and my prized Californian Lotus Cortina, which I had sold to him shortly before David Sutton Motorsport went into administration, he also set us to work restoring some of the vehicles from his collection, starting with a Lancia Stratos. Like most of his other classic rally cars, this was eventually to end up in our museum.

Despite the fact that he spoke barely a word of English while I had only a smattering of schoolboy Spanish, Ignacio and I hit it off right from the start and he soon became not just my most important client but also a close personal friend, as did his partner, wealthy Venezuelan businesswoman Ana Goni. An all-action type who enjoys scuba diving and who even did a bit of sky diving in her youth, Ana also shared Ignacio's passion for rallysport and it was this that had brought them together.

They had been shocked to find us operating out of a farmyard following the collapse of David Sutton Motorsport. Apart from the fact that this gave the appearance of being less than entirely professional, with extremely valuable specialist cars being worked on under the very noses of horses gazing out of stable doors, the very basic working conditions were far from ideal in the unheated garage, especially with winter approaching.

Ignacio urged us to get a proper workshop and, being well aware of the very difficult circumstances in which we found ourselves, offered to pay the first year's rent. This was an arrangement that obviously suited me very well. We went out and found an ideal place in north Daventry, not far from where David Sutton Motorsport had been previously, and started settling in.

When, a few months later, the farm was eventually sold, leaving Jill and I homeless, Ignacio again came to the rescue. As we drove away from the house for the last time, Jill was in tears. The moment had been given added poignancy by a document we had received from the bank that morning. This gave a detailed breakdown of the figures relating to the winding down of the business and the sale of all our assets, including the house. The bottom line read simply: Balance due to Mr and Mrs D. Sutton - £0.00.

My humble plea to the bank to let us have maybe £10,000 to put towards the deposit on a house or an apartment fell on deaf ears. They wouldn't consider it. Meanwhile, Ignacio and Ana had asked us to look out for a house that they could buy and use as a base on their regular visits to England and when Jill found them a very nice property in nearby Priors Marston they kindly invited us to live there ourselves and look after it for them. We have remained there to this day, while Ana later bought a second house just across the road.

With a new workshop and a new motorsport enterprise that was beginning to pick up nicely, the dark clouds that had hung over me during the final traumatic years of David Sutton Motorsport at last began to lift.

With Historic Motorsport I basically started again from scratch as a Jack-of-all-trades, helping out wherever I was needed. I did all the paperwork, bought and collected all the parts from the suppliers and regularly drove backwards and forwards to Spain to pick up the cars from Ignacio's large collection that he wanted us to restore and service, getting to know the road from Daventry to his home in Hondaribbia so well that I think I probably could have driven it blindfold.

For the next couple of years, Ignacio rallied all over Europe in the Mini and the Lotus Cortina and also in a big Mercedes 220 SE that we prepared especially for the 1994 Historic Monte Carlo. After several quite reasonable results, including 7th overall in the 1000 Lakes, he recorded his first Historic win in the West Cork Rally of that year.

At this point he decided that he would like to do one of the more classic regularity events and so we entered him for the Pirelli Classic Marathon from Paris to Marrakesh. Having had no previous experience of regularity rallying, he and his co-driver, a young Spaniard from Barcelona named Francisco Bofill, came over to England for a weekend of intensive training and preparation that included late night dummy runs through the leafy lanes of Warwickshire, complete with pre-arranged control points.

At the last moment tragedy then struck completely out of the blue when we received the shock news that Francisco was dead. Apparently overwhelmed by various personal problems of which we had had no inkling beforehand, this charming young man had, sadly, taken his own life.

Ignacio having resolved after much heart-searching to go ahead with the rally, Francisco's place in the navigator's seat was taken, at very short notice, by David Nicholson. The only real problem here was one of communication, since Ignacio still spoke virtually no English. David, however, sat down with a dictionary and a Spanish phrase book and did three days of intensive homework at the end of which he had a crib sheet that he reckoned would enable him to cover every eventuality.

A serious misunderstanding nevertheless arose on the first regularity section. This took place at night, starting in Nimes. Inside the car it must have been like one of those scenes from Fawlty Towers, featuring Basil Fawlty and Spanish waiter Manuel, as David tried to convey that they were running behind schedule and needed to make up time, only for Ignacio to interpret his pidgin Spanish to mean exactly the opposite.

By the time they got to the end of the stage they were 47 seconds behind and way back in the field. Fortunately, Ana Goni, who speaks perfect English, had also entered the event in a Mini Cooper, with Pauline Gullick as her co-driver, and she soon managed to sort out the confusion when they met up at the rest halt. From then on Ignacio and David started moving up through the field.

The next crisis came in Spain when the gearbox started to disintegrate. At the end of that day the ever resourceful David Nicholson jacked the car up in the hotel car park and stood it on spare tyres borrowed from fellow competitors while he stripped the box down, only to find that 3rd gear had lost all its teeth.

Along with mechanic Tony Devantier, I was shadowing the rally from a distance of about 100 miles when David rang us to explain what had happened and to seek advice. Having asked Tony to tell him exactly how many teeth there should be, he then very carefully drained and washed out the case until he was satisfied that he had found and removed every last one before re-assembling it, enabling them to drive the rest of the rally with just the three gears.

Although no organised service was allowed on the event, it was quite within the regulations for me to shadow the cars from a distance in this way and to offer advice over the phone. There was an amusing moment at a later stage in the rally when the event organiser, Philip Young, a wily old bird who knew me well and half-suspected that I might be much closer than I actually was, stood chatting to Ana and Pauline as they waited for the cars to be ferried across from Algeciras to Tangier for the Moroccan section. "Come on, admit it – I know Sutton's got to be here somewhere," he said, glancing warily around. "I can sense his presence!" At that precise moment a helicopter flew over. "Well, talk of the devil!" joked Ana as they all looked up simultaneously.

I had predicted that if Ignacio were to be anywhere in the Top Ten by the time he reached Morocco, then he would stand a very good chance of winning. I had good reason to feel confident. The organisers had billed the event as being much rougher and tougher than it actually was and many of the competitors had been persuaded to set up their cars accordingly, with heavy-duty off-road tyres and an excess of spares. Between us, however, David Nicholson and I had had a lot of experience in the Middle East and we reckoned that the terrain on this particular event, even in the brief but much-hyped Sahara sections, would not be that rugged and that if you knew how to read the desert you might even be able to take some short cuts without risking excessive tread wear. We therefore decided to use tarmac tyres rather than gravel or desert tyres and travelled light on spares and high on clearance.

It was a gamble that paid off in spectacular fashion. Ignacio was lying sixth at the start of the desert stage and, taking a straight line cross country rather than following the marked track, he passed two of the cars ahead of him without even seeing them! He was fourth fastest through the desert – on tarmac tyres.

From then on it was pretty much plain sailing. In front of him were a Ford Zephyr, a Triumph TR3 and an MGB all of whom must have thought they had it made once they reached the first long tarmac special stage. However, with their heavy-duty gravel tyres and relatively low-slung suspension they could manage no more than about 70mph on the bumpy, single-lane tarmac surface and Ignacio almost literally kicked sand in their faces, racing past, just off-road, at 100 mph. Passing the Zephyr after it had spun, he took a lead he never thereafter surrendered.

Ana and Pauline, meanwhile, had not fared quite so well in the Mini Cooper. Going through the Todra Gorge they hit another competitor, who had come round a corner on the wrong side of the road, and lost a lot of time as a result. Despite this accident, they struggled on gamely and still had the considerable satisfaction of managing to qualify as finishers, much to the relief of Ignacio, who, in typically gentlemanly fashion, had been more concerned about Ana's progress than about his own.

For Historic Motorsport, his win was a landmark victory that put us right back on the map. But then, just a few weeks later, came an announcement that sealed our return even more emphatically.

MARATHON MAN

When Nick Brittan's Transworld Events organisation announced in July 1994 that they were going to stage a 25th anniversary re-run of the 1970 London-Mexico Rally, Ford immediately contacted the original winners, Hannu Mikkola and his co-driver Gunnar Palm, to ask if they would be interested in trying to repeat their famous victory. Hannu replied that they would be delighted to have a go on one condition – that Ford asked David Sutton to build the car.

This was a great honour and a huge compliment. Coming from the man universally acknowledged to have been one of the best rally drivers of all time, if not the best ever, it was a vote of confidence that not only provided one of the proudest moments of my life, but which also worked wonders for the reputation of Historic Motorsport. Suddenly, we were back representing a leading manufacturer, with a legendary, world-class driver. After all that Jill and I had been through in the previous couple of years, this gave us an enormous fillip.

As soon as the word got around that we were preparing the official Works car for Ford and Hannu, we promptly sold two more Escorts to Richard Martin-Hurst and Sandy Delgano. At the same time, Ignacio, who had no wish to be left out of such a prestigious event, but who wanted to do it in a more leisurely style, asked me to prepare a 6.3 litre V8 Mercedes from his collection. This, unfortunately, was destined to be probably the most troublesome car I have ever prepared in my entire motorsport career, as we shall see later!

Meanwhile, I had re-connected with Ford Boreham for initial discussions to find that only two of the people who had been involved with me in the original event, under Stuart Turner, were still there in the competitions department. One of them was my old friend Bill Meade, who, to my great delight, was immediately assigned to work with us on the project.

Ford's first thought was to use Hannu's original 1970 winning car, FEV 1H, which was in their museum. There were obvious PR advantages to be gained from this, but after a closer look at the regulations, and given the fact that certain materials had improved considerably during the intervening twenty-five years, they came to the conclusion that it would be necessary to build a more powerful, long-distance marathon car if we wanted to have any chance of winning.

With plenty of time to spare, having announced our entry very early, we had the luxury of being able to build the car slowly and carefully, carrying out some fairly comprehensive testing in Wales along the way. We also arranged to run it as a course opening car on the 1994 RAC Rally, a useful opportunity for Hannu to familiarise himself with the car in actual rally conditions.

One of the special modifications to the car of which we were particularly proud was a twin fuel tank system that we had developed to deal with the problem of low-grade South American petrol, known less than affectionately to one and all as "Paraguayan Parrot Piss". In some places this can be as low as 80-octane.

The idea behind our twin-tank arrangement was that it would enable you to fill one tank with high-octane aviation fuel begged from local airfields along the route, mixing this with regular low-octane stuff from the other tank to produce an acceptable blend. We included the further refinement of a dump valve on the bottom of each tank so that if you happened to find yourself in a situation where you had been forced to make do with two tanks of the local stuff shortly before chancing upon an obliging airfield, you could quickly drain one tank and refill it with Avgas. As we were to discover, not even this could prevent problems with Brazil's sugar-based fuel.

London-Mexico did not allow any organised service, a mistake in my view. This ruling caused problems for many competitors while encouraging some Teams to resort to underhand methods, not so say downright cheating, in order to maintain and service their cars en route.

Pre-positioning of spare parts and materials for the event was, however, permitted and shortly before the start on April 22nd, 1995, I set off on a whistle-stop tour of Ford importers in Paraguay, Bolivia, Peru, Panama and Mexico to carry out a recce and make sure that all the necessary arrangements had been agreed and were in place. These involved sending out crates of the heavier spare parts such as drive shafts and suspension units, together with extra wheels and tyres, which would then be positioned at four or five-day intervals, ready for Hannu and Gunnar to carry out their own repairs, if necessary.

If they happened to suffer a major failure in between they would either have to carry out some sort of temporary bush repair to hold them until they got to the next spares dump or they would have to retire. Or they could possibly try to take advantage of a rather vague rule stating that a car could be towed by a fellow competitor 'for a reasonable distance'.

That great character, the late and much lamented Charles Golding, was rumoured to have exploited this slight ambiguity during the 2000 London-Sydney to the extent of being towed by a team-mate for almost the entire rally! A seriously quick driver at his best, Charles was also a fearsomely determined competitor who would never give up and I can imagine that the story is probably true. Crowned Historic British Rally Champion in 2002, only months before his death, he was a wonderfully ebullient, larger-than-life personality with a great sense of fun and is sadly missed by all of us who knew him and were entertained by him.

I was accompanied on the reconnaissance trip by my old friend and former Team driver Mike Hibbert, who happened to be free at the time and, having never been to South America before, fancied coming with me to have a look around. The expedition turned out to be a bit more adventurous than anticipated as we raced around at the rate of a country-per-day, travelling mostly in the same ancient Boeing 737.

We held our breath every time the 30-year-old aircraft struggled into the air. At high altitude locations like La Paz, especially, it really laboured to get off the ground in the thin atmosphere, everyone on board going very quiet as we seriously began to wonder if we were ever going to make it. And on one occasion the pilot apparently grew tired of waiting for his departure slot and simply jumped the queue, bumping across the grass and onto the adjoining runway to make a quick getaway. All this is fairly typical of air travel South American style.

Fortunately, the stewardesses served us enormous amounts of booze on these internal flights, which helped to steady the nerves. Mike, however, was not at all put at his ease by my repeated assurances that everything would be OK. He recalled that in the days when he had been driving for me on a regular basis he had learned to be deeply suspicious whenever I came up to him at a service point and put an arm round his shoulder as I steered him towards a car that he wasn't totally happy about with the words: "Trust me, Michael – the car's all right."

"I always knew then that there was almost certainly something fiercely wrong with it that you weren't going to tell me about," he said anxiously.

Elsewhere in South America, our arrival in Tuxtla Gutierrez in Mexico coincided with a minor palace coup. We couldn't understand why our hotel was completely empty until we glanced out of the window at breakfast the next morning to see tanks patrolling the streets. But at least we had the hotel swimming pool to ourselves, giggling like schoolboys over a sign that warned: 'No Farting In Pool'.

We ended the trip with a few very pleasant days in Acapulco, one of my favourite places in the world. I had thoroughly enjoyed having Mike along for company. He remains one of the best of the old school, a naturally gifted driver with a wonderfully laid-back manner and a droll sense of humour. I was delighted when, very shortly after our South American odyssey, he agreed to come out of retirement to drive a series of Historic events for me.

Following the formal unveiling of the car and the official announcement of Hannu's and Gunnar's participation at the annual Ford Motorsport press conference in Zurich in January 1995, excitement began to mount steadily as we approached the start of the month-long rally.

Although some 4,000km shorter than the 24,000km 1970 original, which had started with an extended European section that took it all the way from London to Sofia and back to Lisbon before sailing from there to Rio to start the South American phase, the altogether more relaxed anniversary event still promised to be a considerable test of physical stamina and mental endurance as well as driving skill and versatility, especially for veterans like Hannu and Gunnar, who were now in their fifties rather than their twenties. Gunnar summed up the difference between the two events very succinctly when he later reflected: "In 1995 it was for human beings, in 1970 it was for madmen."

Organised to coincide with soccer's World Cup Finals in Mexico, the original had been only the second-ever marathon after the 1968 London-Sydney and with single stages of up to 1,000km and sections in the Andes that took it to altitudes where the drivers were advised to carry oxygen in the cars, it was far tougher than anything that had gone before.

With seven Escorts in the event, including the one that Clarke & Simpson had prepared for Rauno Aaltonen and another in which England soccer star Jimmy Greaves accompanied Tony Fall as a celebrity co-driver, Ford had invested in a vast amount of advance preparation. Gunnar had been sent to do exactly the same sort of pre-event reconnaissance tour of South American importers that I did in 1995 and, along with Tony Fall, had also taken part in the 1969 Camino del Incas in a Works-prepared car in order to assess the special problems of driving at altitude.

At anything above 4,000 metres, both cars and drivers can be affected, the cars losing power and drivers finding it increasingly difficult to measure distances and perspective, a considerable disadvantage when you're going flat out through the mountains with a sheer drop on one side! Because they were in the lead, Hannu and Gunnar, in 1970, threw out their oxygen cylinders to save weight, gambling on the fact that with so many team mates coming up behind them they could always borrow a whiff or two from them if necessary.

Many pictures taken during the event show drivers with oxygen masks and Jimmy Greaves famously fainted as he got out of his car in La Paz and stepped forward to be interviewed for television. Fortunately, Hannu and Gunnar never experienced any problems in this respect, despite reaching altitudes of nearly 5,000 metres at the highest point, between Cuzco and Huancayo in Peru.

It was on this 961 km stage, which didn't figure in the 1995 event, that Hannu produced what Gunnar rates as one of the most extraordinary driving feats of all time. Starting early in the morning, he went flat out for twelve hours twenty-three minutes, virtually non-stop. There were just three short breaks – the first when they had to repair a broken throttle linkage, using a rubber band; the second when they refuelled at around the halfway point and gobbled two hard-boiled eggs washed down with Coca Cola; and the third, twenty minutes from the finish, when they had a double puncture. By then, all the tyres were down to the canvas. And still they went as fast as they dared, with terrifying drops on either side of the road at some points and no Armco or safety rail of any kind.

By the time they reached the control point in Huancayo, Hannu was so completely and utterly exhausted that he had to ask Gunnar had to take over and drive the 60km down to the hotel in Lima. With this truly stunning performance he had beaten his nearest rival by more than twenty minutes, delivering the knock out punch that laid the foundation of his eventual victory.

Could he and Gunnar repeat their triumph twenty-five years later? The omens were not good when they started having engine problems fairly early on. As the Team Manager on an event like this you feel rather helpless, sitting at home on the end of a phone, trying to direct things by remote control. By the time they reached South America the calls were coming in at all hours of the day and night. These would often involve requests for extra spares and on one occasion we actually flew Mike Hibbert out from London to Peru with the vital part under his arm rather than trying to send it out as cargo. It would never have made it through the Peruvian customs in time!

The first major crisis came in Brazil when the poor quality petrol literally brought the engine problems to a head with the failure of the head gasket. Marooned in the middle of a sugar plantation, miles from anywhere, we were in danger of being forced to retire until we had the first of several strokes of luck with the arrival on the scene of Sandy Delgano and his co-driver Sandy Taylor, who were both experienced mechanics and who very sportingly stopped to assist. As it happened, Hannu and Gunnar had already given 'the two Sandys', as they were known to one and all, a bit of help and advice earlier on and so they were happy to return the favour, even though it cost them a couple of hours. With long distances between each special stage they were able to make up this lost time without too much difficulty.

This roadside repair held until Hannu and Gunnar reached Asuncion in Paraguay when the gasket once again sprang a leak, causing the engine to overheat. Here they had an even greater bit of luck when the cavalry came riding to their rescue in the shape of George Botha. George was a former mechanic of mine who had gone with us to Paraguay for an event some years before and, having been left behind to clear up afterwards, had fallen in love with a local girl, married her and never returned, going on to become the technical engineer and manager for the local Toyota Rally Team. He was conveniently on hand when Hannu and Gunnar limped into the control point and very kindly offered to sort the problem out for them while they grabbed some well-earned sleep.

All his good work was then very nearly undone when Hannu and Gunnar, forgetting that they had crossed into a new time zone between Brazil and Paraguay and having not reset their watches, got up an hour late and had to drive flat out through Asuncion in the rush hour to get to the starting line in time, eventually making it with only minutes to spare. From then on their progress was fairly uneventful until they got to Colombia, where they were advised to travel in convoy at one point to minimise the risk of attack by bandits!

Ignacio, meanwhile, had started off very well in the big Mercedes, which was probably the most powerful car in the entire field. As he went through France and Spain and into Portugal he was up among the leaders, somewhere in the Top Ten. However, he then started having problems with the brakes, the suspension and the automatic transmission and was finally forced to retire in Brazil. The car was never right and I have to put up my hands and admit that we may have been guilty of being so much in awe of preparing the Works car for Ford that we didn't give the Mercedes quite the detailed attention it deserved.

Although disappointed at being out of the rally, Ignacio soon recovered his usual good spirits and after having the car repaired locally in Brazil he then motored up to Acapulco for the finish and, more important, the end-of-rally party.

I had flown in with Ford's Director of Motorsport, Martin Whitaker, to watch Hannu and Gunnar cross the finishing line in style on May 21st, exactly one month after leaving London. Back in 1970 they had been given a motorcycle escort for the last few kilometres into the Azteca Stadium, which was to be the venue for the World Cup Final shortly afterwards. Here they were accorded a heroes' welcome, formally greeted by various sporting celebrities. The reception they got in 1995 was a little less grand, but for Gunnar, who had not been actively involved in rallying of any sort since his retirement twenty-three years previously in 1972, it was a very emotional moment and he wept unashamedly, tears of joy and relief at what had been a magnificent achievement. There were one or two others amongst us who were moist-eyed but Hannu, as ever, remained characteristically cool, calm and collected, as if it were all in a day's work.

Returning to England after a few days' holiday in Acapulco with Ignacio, I decided to throw a celebration party at home in Priors Marston. Having been in the doldrums since the demise of David Sutton Motorsport, it was simply marvellous to have something to shout about. Led by Hannu and Gunnar, a host of celebrities turned up to share our delight at being well and truly back in business. Also wheeled out for the occasion were the two winning London-Mexico Escorts, 1970's FEV 1H and – a lovely touch, this – 1995's specially registered H1 FEV.

Andy Anderson, the PR consultant responsible for handling all Ford's Press and public relations work for the rally, had pulled off a fantastic publicity coup in managing to purchase this valuable and wonderfully appropriate registration. With a bit of delicate but perfectly legal paperwork it had been assigned to the 1995 car, providing a neatly symmetrical touch to a memorable triumph.

All that remained to be done, once the dust had finally settled, was for me to revisit the South American importers to organise the safe return of all the spare parts, wheels, tyres and other material that had been sent out but not used. This time I took with me another old friend, Ian 'Del' Lines and, once again, it was a most enjoyable trip – although the task of negotiating the passage of all our scattered bits and pieces through the complexities of South American Customs bureaucracy was to prove quite a challenge, especially in the case of one crate of spares – the most valuable, needless to say! – which did not finally arrive back in the UK until a year later.

After all the excitement of London-Mexico there was obviously a risk that the rest of 1995 might turn out to be a bit of an anti-climax, but any chance of this happening was removed when, only days after our return from Acapulco, Mike Hibbert went out to record a famous victory in the Scottish Historic Rally.

It had been twenty-two years since Mike had last driven a rally car in anger but it was as if he had never been away and his performance drew a rave review from John Fife in Motoring News. Equally impressed was his co-driver Dave Cabena, who later described in graphic detail how, as they went flat out through the forest, he had looked across to see Mike "dancing on the pedals", his hands clear of the wheel as he controlled the car with his feet alone.

His good form continued in Finland where he came fifth overall and might have done even better had he been supplied with the right tyres. At least, that's his story! The way I remember it, he was lucky to have got as far as the start line.

He had flown to Helsinki with Dave Cabena and I and as he and I between us had done a pretty good job of emptying the plane's grog cupboard on the way over, Dave volunteered to drive up to Jyväskylä. Mike wouldn't hear of it and insisted on taking the wheel himself on the grounds that he needed as much experience as possible driving on the wrong side of the road.

As it was getting late and the roads were pretty clear Mike soon had the pedal to the metal. We were about an hour into our journey before we encountered the first car coming in the opposite direction and because we were doing about 110 mph it wasn't unti too late that we realised it was a police car.

The penalties in Finland for any kind of driving offence are draconian - especially when it comes to even the mildest drink driving offence - so there was then a discussion about whether we should try to outrun the police car, which had immediately done a U-turn and was now chasing us with lights flashing and siren blaring. The worry was that if Mike were found to be over the limit by even the smallest amount he was likely to be sent to prison and, apart from anything else, that would have meant a wasted journey for all of us.

In the end we decided this wasn't an option, but as we pulled over I opened all the windows, fed Mike some Polo mints and warned him in no way to reveal that he was a rally driver, since the Finnish police regarded all rally drivers as hooligans. "Tell them we are on a fishing expedition," I hissed. Mike listened to all this and then got out and walked back to the police car where he discovered, to his delight, that the crew consisted of two extremely attractive blonde policewomen.

Mike's undoubted appeal to members of the opposite sex has always been something of a mystery to his fellow men. Let's face it, we are not talking George Clooney here! Anyway, turning on all his legendary, snake-like charm, he chatted these two WPC's up for about 20 minutes at the end of which they were giggling like schoolgirls and were positively apologetic as they explained that they had no option but to fine him the equivalent of about £300 for the speeding offence. To top it off, they wished him good fishing, adding that they were hoping to be in Jyväskylä over the weekend and looked forward to the possibility of bumping into him again.

Lo and behold, they did just that. Driving into a main time control in a village where the local mayor, the local beauty queen and a choir had all turned out to greet the cars, Mike was about to make a play for the beauty queen when he suddenly spotted the two policewomen heading straight for him. "Enjoying the fishing trip?" they smiled sweetly. And then, looking in my direction, they added" "You should have told us you were a rally driver with David Sutton. Don't bother paying the fine. Just give us the ticket and we will tear it up."

I had been kidding Mike that I was a national hero in Finland because of my many successes with Finnish drivers over the years, but even I didn't really believe it until that moment.

As for the rally itself, I have to admit that my choice of tyres was not too good on this occasion, having opted for mud and snow tyres when everybody else was on intermediates. Almost the exact reverse was true a few weeks later on the Historic RAC. As they were about to set off from Leeds, Dave Cabena sniffed the air and said that he could smell snow. "Trust me," I said dismissively, putting an arm around Mike's shoulder and no doubt striking a chill into his heart once again. "There's no snow about and you'll be fine on regular tyres." I should have relied more on Yorkshireman Dave Cabena's local knowledge because no sooner had they got into the Dales than the first flakes started to fall!

With the momentum from our high profile London-Mexico win continuing to build, we entered a full programme of Historic events in 1996, opening with the Monte Carlo Challenge. This was the first year in which we enjoyed what was to become a regular annual invasion of wealthy Americans and Canadians, who came over with the sole intention of renting a car, driving to Monte Carlo and having a great time before flying home again. On this occasion we had a selection of millionaire businessmen from New York, San Diego and Thunder Bay in Canada and, partly in order to keep a close eye on the proceedings, I decided to do the event myself in a Mini Cooper S with Pauline Gullick as my co-driver.

Pauline has been involved with us right from the very earliest days of David Sutton Motorsport in 1975 when she became Jill's co-driver for the Sherry Rally in Spain, one of the first events we did after setting up the company. While working as a PR for the Prison Service – and suffering, with patient good humour, all the bad jokes that inevitably tend to come her way as a result – she had begun her career as a navigator with Rosemary Smith, meeting up with Jill and I when we were still at Clarke &

The mighty bucking Bronco on high-speed desert manouevres and (bottom left) Saeed Al Hajri holds the reins as co-driver Steve Bond test drives a more sedate means of transport.

Flying royal visit from King Hussein's son Prince Feisal, (centre) at a service point in Jordan.

One of the burnt out service vans in Kuwait following the Iraqi invasion.

Ignacio Sunsundequi taking a breather during the Paris-Marrakesh Pirelli Classic and (right) the remains of his Mini Cooper after a slight indiscretion on the Circuit of Ireland!

Jill and I get into the spirit of things for an Arabian night out to celebrate my 50th in Dubai (below left) and (below right) with my late stepson, Guy.

Ana Goni and the late Ignacio Sunsundegui, clients and mentors who, between them, did so much to help me to get back on my feet after the disasters of 1992.

Ignacio on the Historic Monte Carlo in one of his collection of Mercedes, with Colin Francis as co-driver and Ana acting as interpreter.

A rare relaxing moment in Finland with (from left) David Nicholson, Ana Goni, Ignacio's late co-driver Francisco Bofill and Ignacio himself.

Ignacio flanked by Roger Clark and Francisco Bofill....

... and (below) on his last rally.

The Historic Motorsport Museum at Daventry where we have more than thirty classic cars.

(Centre) The Volvo PV544 as I found it in an orchard in California and as it is now, after one of our best ever restoration projects.

Hannu Mikkola's Audi LYV 4X,(right), probably the world's most photographed rally car.

Juha and Hannu Mikkola with Mitsubishi's Andrew Cowan at the start of the 2000 London-Sydney Marathon ....and on their way (right)

(Left to Right) Bjorn Waldegard, Stig Blomqvist and Hannu Mikkola at the Goodwood Festival of Speed with the 1995 London-Mexico Escort H1 FEV in the background.

Stig Blomqvist and Ana Goni in action in Cyprus (above) and (left) getting us off to a winning start with Subaru in the 2003 Swedish Rally.

John Lloyd comparing notes with co-driver Pauline Gullick (below)

With four of ' my' World Champions. (l to r) Bjorn Waldegard, Hannu Mikkola, Ari Vatanen and Stig Blomqvist.

Happy birthday boy with Jill, Ana and present.

(Below left) Stig and Ana at the 2002 Network Q and (below right) grandson Jamie showing driving ambition at the Rally of Finland.

Simpson. Apart from Jill, with whom she regularly drove in events all over the world, she has, at various times, partnered Jimmy McRae, Pentti Airikkala, Michele Mouton ... and me.

On this occasion we made an inglorious early exit. It was so freezing cold that after getting off the boat in Calais and starting to drive down through France we could barely see where we were going because the windscreen kept icing up on the inside. And then the engine blew up, forcing our retirement.

The week before this event I had had the sad duty of attending Jim Dewar's funeral. Originally a private client back in the Clarke & Simpson days, Jim went on to become a good friend and played a key role on two occasions in my career, first providing the financial backing that enabled me to set up David Sutton (Cars) Ltd and, later, helping to negotiate the World Championship-winning contract with Rothmans.

Jim, who ran his own hugely successful accountancy practice, had been a high flier in those days, a larger-than-life character and a real showman who certainly didn't fit the traditional, rather dull image of an accountant. But then things started to go wrong. An expensive divorce was followed by ruinous business problems and, next thing I knew, Jim had been found dead in his car at a remote spot on the Yorkshire Moors. It was a bleak moment.

My spirits received a welcome boost shortly after this when Jimmy McRae, driving our Lotus Cortina, won both the Welsh and Scottish Historic Rallies within the space of a few weeks, providing a superb demonstration of how a conventional rear wheel drive Historic rally car could beat even the mighty Porsches.

Five times a winner of the British Rally Championship and with three consecutive Scottish Historic Rally victories also to his credit, Jimmy deserved wider recognition for his talents. Unfortunately, his contract with Vauxhall confined him to the British Championship in such a way that he never really had the opportunity to make a name for himself on the world stage. As quiet and easy-going as Colin is volatile and extreme, Jimmy made sure that his sons didn't miss out in the same way.

Elsewhere during 1996, Ignacio was delighted to win the Targa Espana in his own back yard, while I myself managed to pull off quite a coup by luring Michele Mouton out of retirement for a one-off appearance at the annual Goodwood Festival of Speed. By regularly attracting an international galaxy of stars and cars of every type and vintage, Lord March, Goodwood's owner, has succeeded in establishing this as one of the biggest and most celebrated gatherings of its kind in the world. From such legendary figures as Sir Stirling Moss and Sir Jack Brabham through to many of today's biggest names from both F1 and the World Rally Championship, the guest list reads like a Who's Who of motorsport.

The event itself is a glorified hill climb, featuring all manner of exotic and historic cars dating from the 1930s onwards. Michele drove our S1 Quattro and gave everyone present a reminder of her phenomenal talents.

As I have already mentioned, she remains by far the greatest lady driver of all time, more than able to hold her own with the men in any situation, as she proved when she came second in the World Championship, only a point or two behind the eventual winner. At the same time, she has never been in the least bit butch' or masculine. On the contrary, she is an extremely attractive woman – every sponsor's dream.

Over the years that I worked with her, I probably got to know Michele as well as anyone and we have remained close friends ever since. She possesses a fiery temperament coupled with great determination and absolutely no fear – a formidable combination in any competitor. But none of this ever showed until the moment that the timekeepers announced: "1-2-3-Go". And then it was as if she sprouted horns and a red mist descended.

Her appearance at Goodwood marked the first time she had been behind the wheel for almost ten years. Having left the Audi team after they withdrew from Group B, she had one season in the German Championship with the revolutionary Peugeot T16 before quitting altogether in her mid-30s. She was still in her prime as a driver, but with the birth of her daughter, Jesse, her priorities changed almost overnight. Jesse was suddenly the only thing that really mattered to her and as her enthusiasm for motorsport waned, she lost that edge that had always set her apart.

Her only regular involvement in motorsport nowadays is with the annual Race of Champions that she stages down in Gran Canaria. A rallysprint competition, this always features many of the great names of the past – the 'Rally Legends' as they are billed. Hannu, Stig, Bjorn Waldegard and the rest all turn up and we usually lend her a few cars from the museum. In 2002 we sent over five, including two Mitsubishis, a Ford RS 200, a Lancia Stratos and an S1 Quattro.

Following the death of Jim Dewar in the early part of the year, I was further saddened in the summer by the announcement that the great Belgian driver, Gilbert Staepelaere, had also died. One of the most talented drivers of all time, Gilbert altogether notched up more than 100 victories for Ford, winning his own home championship no less than eight times. I had the pleasure of building a number of his cars in the days of David Sutton Cars and had got to know him well and to like him enormously. His passing came as a shock.

There was some better news later in the year with the announcement by Transworld Events of another major marathon rally – this time from Panama to Alaska. I was immediately asked to prepare two cars – one, as usual, for Ignacio and another for an exciting new private client, John Lloyd.

A senior partner in Jardine Lloyd Thompson, one of the world's leading insurance brokerage companies, John had first been introduced to us by Pauline Gullick, who had been co-driving for him in club events since 1993 and who later went on to become his full time rally co-ordinator. He had been born and brought up in Africa, where his father, an executive with international car dealers Inchcape, was a keen motorsport enthusiast who had been involved in the organisation of the old original East African Safari Rally, often taking young John along to help him man the control points. As a result, John had had an interest in rallying from an early age but had been too busy building a successful, high-flying City career to be able to get seriously into the sport until relatively late in life, being almost into his forties before he found the time to start rallying Austin Healeys, Ferraris and an Aston Martin DB6 in regularity events in this country.

A hugely energetic and very determined character, he soon got bored with this rather low-key level of competition and decided that he wanted to move up a few gears to special stage events, starting with a crack at the Historic Rally Championship. It was then that Pauline brought him to us.

Having never driven a yard of gravel at this point, he asked me to arrange a discreet event where he could learn about the car and get some experience of driving in those conditions. I selected the Rally Reykavik in Iceland in September 1996 as being ideal. For good measure, I also entered two Lotus Cortinas for Ignacio and Mike Hibbert in addition to John's Escort.

This turned out to be a huge success in every respect. Scenically, Iceland is a pretty God-forsaken place. Flat in every direction, with very few trees, it's a bit like being on the moon – but the roads are very interesting, the surfaces being mostly black volcanic gravel that spreads right over the verges and banks, making it very difficult to find the right line through the corners. With a lawyer friend, Paul Amandini, as co-driver, John nevertheless won his post-Historic class in the Escort and with Ignacio and Mike also doing well in their class, we returned with an impressive selection of trophies.

It is the only event I have ever been involved in where even the mechanics are called up on stage to receive awards. Add to this the fact that the Icelandic people in general are the friendliest you will meet anywhere in the world and that the girls all seem to be stunning – I once heard a Miss World winner admit that she had managed only sixth place in a Reykavik beauty contest – and you can understand why we all came back wreathed in smiles.

Flush with success, we next entered John in the Historic RAC in a Cortina borrowed from Mike Hibbert, but this literally brought him down to earth with a bang as he proceeded to roll the car twice within the first twenty-four hours, prompting Pauline Gullick, back in the co-driver's seat for this event, to suggest that enough was enough and that it was maybe time to retire gracefully. For Mike Hibbert, ruefully inspecting the damage, insult was added to injury when he returned to the car park to find that the car he had driven up in had been broken into and vandalised.

Meanwhile, in October, I had decided to visit a number of Ford dealers in the USA, Canada and Alaska to arrange for the pre-positioning of spare parts, wheels and tyres for the forthcoming Panama-Alaska, just as I had done for the London-Mexico. And, again, I was accompanied by 'Del' Lines.

Del and I go back to my very earliest days in Mansfield and, in fact, it was he who loaned me one of his vans in which to transport my belongings to London when I moved down in 1966. By way of return, he credits me with providing the inspiration that prompted him to follow his heart and quit the rather boring security of the hosiery business in favour of a far more rewarding career restoring performance cars.

With Del reading the maps and me behind the wheel of a Toyota Camry, we set off to drive from Las Vegas right up to Anchorage, via the Alaska Highway. The total distance amounted to over 3,000 miles – and I have to say that it was one of the hairiest and most exciting trips I've ever undertaken.

I had been advised that we needed to get to Canada no later than the first week in November if we wanted to beat the onset of winter, but made the mistake of therefore assuming that everything would be fine in mid-October. Wrong. Temperatures had already plummeted by then, snow had started to fall and several of the more remote mountain roads were blocked, while even the main highways were like skating rinks.

On top of that, we regularly encountered an additional and unexpected local hazard. Nothing quite prepares you for the first time you come over the crest of a hill on a dead straight road to find yourself suddenly having to slalom through a kerb-to-kerb herd of migrating caribou. We had several near misses.

One way and another it was a memorable experience, our itinerary taking us through a whole string of locations with names like Dawson Creek, Watson Lake and Whitehorse. And the Ford dealers we visited along the way were all extremely enthusiastic, saying how much they were looking forward to the arrival of our cars the following year.

Sadly, this was never going to happen.

ANNUS HORRIBILIS

All the signs were that 1997 was going to be one of the best years ever for Historic Motorsport. We had announced that we would be entering no less than three Lotus Cortinas in the Historic Rally Championship, one to be driven by Jimmy McRae and the other two by Mike Hibbert and John Lloyd. Also in our programme was the Historic Safari Rally, with John Lloyd in his fabulous Ford Escort RS 1600, followed in mid-summer by the main event, the eagerly awaited Panama-Alaska.

At the same time, with Ignacio's enthusiastic backing, we had started looking around for bigger and better premises in Daventry in which to accommodate our rapidly expanding business that by now was starting to burst at the seams. One way and another it seemed that we had every reason to welcome the New Year in bullish mood, without the slightest indication that all our high hopes and expectations were soon to be shattered in the most devastating fashion.

There was an early disappointment when John Lloyd was forced out of the Historic Safari after getting stuck in sand while lying 2nd. Unfortunately, he then had to cancel his plans to join Ignacio in the Panama-Alaska when a major business merger involving his company prevented him from taking that amount of time away from the office.

Ignacio, with partner Ana Goni as his co-driver, was meanwhile greatly looking forward to the event in the confident hope of improving on his previous marathon performance in the 1995 London-Mexico. We shipped his Escort out to Panama along with a Ford Explorer service and support vehicle and one of my senior technicians, Gareth Williams, and I myself then flew out for a couple of days to make a final check on all the arrangements before seeing Ignacio and Ana off with the promise that I would be there to meet them when they arrived at the extended rest halt in Las Vegas two weeks later. That done, I then got straight on a plane and returned to the UK to supervise our entries in the Historic Scottish Rally.

I arrived home on the morning of June 3rd, Jill's birthday, delighted that for once in a hectic, globetrotting schedule that has caused me to miss far too many birthdays and anniversaries, I was actually going to be around so that we could celebrate together. Having grabbed a few hours' sleep to refresh myself after the fifteen-hour flight, I took her out to dinner at our favourite restaurant, the Butcher's Arms, less than five minutes' drive up the road in the next village.

The precise events of the next few hours are burnished indelibly on my memory. Having been greeted with the usual warm welcome from proprietor Lino Pires, his wife Augusta and son Peter, we had barely started our meal when the head waiter came over to say that an urgent message had been received requesting me to return home immediately to take an important call from America.

I had grown fairly used to this sort of thing over the years, especially when marathon rallies were in progress. During the 1995 London-Mexico event, Hannu and Gunnar had constantly been on the phone at all hours of the day and night with frantic requests for technical support, for extra spares to be flown out and for help with all manner of other logistical crises.

My first thought was that there must obviously be a problem with Ignacio's car and, leaving Jill sitting in the restaurant, I hurried home, keeping my fingers crossed that it would prove to be nothing too serious. I couldn't imagine, for instance, that they would have crashed out so early on.

The news, when it came, was much worse than that. Almost as soon as I walked through the door the call came through from Los Angeles and somebody I didn't know on the other end of the line explained that he was relaying a message from Costa Rica and very much regretted to have to inform me that Ignacio Sunsundegui had died. He had no other details but had been given a number for me to ring. I dialled it out in a state of shock and was surprised when, after just a couple of rings, the phone was answered by Gareth Williams in person.

I had reached him at the local hospital in Costa Rica, he told me. Clearly very shaken, he then went on to explain that Ignacio had pulled into the service area at the end of a special stage, had got out of the car to stretch his legs and had immediately collapsed, having suffered a massive heart attack. All attempts to revive him had failed and he had died on the spot.

As I struggled to come to terms with this shattering news, I told Gareth to do whatever he could to comfort Ana and promised that I would be on the next available flight out of London. I then rang the Butcher's Arms to say that I would not be returning and would they put Jill in a taxi. Lino himself took care of everything in his usual kindly fashion and when Jill arrived a few minutes later to find me in tears she knew instantly that something terrible had happened.

It was now about 11.00pm, too late to speak to my travel agent. I phoned British Airways and, of course, their offices were also closed, but I was automatically transferred to a call centre in the USA. I explained that I urgently needed to book a seat on the first flight to Costa Rica, but then realised that, having paid the Team's fairly hefty hotel bill in Panama only the day before, I probably didn't have enough credit left on my card to pay for the ticket. To my great relief, the transaction went through without a hitch, but from that day to this I have always taken the precaution of carrying one extra card with a zero balance, just in case a similar emergency should arise in future.

Still jet-lagged from the previous day's flight, I hurriedly re-packed my bag and set off for Heathrow at about 4.30 a.m. After another gloomy 15-hour flight, I touched down in San Jose and went immediately to the hotel, where Ana and Gareth were awaiting my arrival, along with several of Ignacio's friends who had already arrived from Spain.

Ana, of course, was absolutely distraught, although bravely trying to keep her emotions under control. Like all of us, she had been totally stunned by the unexpected suddenness of it all. There had been absolutely no indication of any problem with Ignacio's health, no sign that he was not feeling himself. Immediately before the event started he had been in his usual jovial high spirits. The post-mortem revealed an oversized heart, which seemed sadly ironic given that here was a man who, in life, had been big hearted in every sense.

Mercifully, in some ways, the speed of the funeral arrangements left us little time to brood too much at this stage on what had happened. It is the custom in Spain to have the interment as soon as possible after death, with the formal funeral service following a few days later, and so, with the help of the Spanish Consulate, arrangements were made to have Ignacio's body flown home for burial the very next day. The rest of us then followed on, gathering in his hometown of Hondarribia for the funeral. Jill, meanwhile, had flown out from England with some of the mechanics to join us there.

Some time later I organised a special memorial service at our village church at home in Priors Marston so that Ignacio's many British friends would have a chance to pay their respects. I had always found it rather ironic that, although he never did learn to speak the language very well, he had a tremendous affection for this country, its people and its traditions. This was reflected in the way that he adopted the style of what he considered to be the true English country gentleman. Always impeccably well-mannered, he would dress in flat cap, tweeds and brogues and Jill was forever giving him gloves, scarves and thick woollen socks as presents, which he loved.

As well as his great generosity, Ignacio possessed tremendous warmth and approachability, which was why he made so many friends wherever he went, especially among the motorsport fraternity. Even so, I was amazed by the response when, with the help of the Historic Rally Car Register and our local vicar, I set about arranging the memorial service.

On the day, St Leonard's Church was packed to overflowing with people who had come from far and wide. That was something you might expect for the likes of Roger Clark or Tony Pond, but for so many drivers, navigators, officials and organisers to take the time and trouble to congregate at a rather remote little country church in honour of a foreign driver who was far from being a big international name struck me as touching tribute to a remarkable man.

His passing left an enormous void in my life in every sense. I had lost not just a true friend, a great mentor and my most important client, but also the investor whose financial backing had enabled me to get back on my feet following the collapse of David Sutton Motorpsort. Without Ignacio's support at that very critical time I doubt whether I would have been able to rebuild my business career quite so successfully, if at all. Now that he was gone, there was, once again, an inevitable question mark over the future.

As it happened, Ana was the one who had actually been putting up most of the money for their joint rallying activities towards the end, but with her insistence, in the immediate aftermath of Ignacio's death, that she herself would never sit in a rally car again, I had to face the distinct possibility that she might lose interest in the sport altogether and end the relationship, in which case there was a danger that the whole business would collapse again..

The immediate situation was complicated by the fact that, at the time of Ignacio's death, we were about to exchange contracts to complete the purchase of the new premises that we had found in Rutherford Way, Daventry and for which the deposit had already been paid.

Painfully aware that it was the wrong time to raise such an issue, and fearful about what the response might be, I had no option but to contact Ana a few days after the funeral to ask her what she wanted to do. Did she still want to go ahead with the move? Or should we just walk away from the deal, which we would have been legally entitled to do at that stage?

To my immense relief, she decided to go ahead. A very wealthy businesswoman in her own right, with extensive family interests in Venezuela, Ana certainly had no plans to continue rallying herself but, at the same time, she saw no reason to withdraw the financial commitment to the company that she had shared with Ignacio. What's more, she already had in the back of her mind the idea of developing part of the site as a rally car museum, dedicated to his memory and housing part of the fabulous collection of cars that he had built up over the years.

With the company's immediate future thus assured, we were able to start planning the new workshops and office while at the same time carrying out the rest of the season's rally programme. However, any hopes we might have had of an early return to normality were almost immediately shattered

Still reeling from the shock of Ignacio's death – and with the entire nation by now in mourning for Princess Diana – Jill and I were hit just weeks later by another tragedy, this time even closer to home. On the day following Diana's funeral, I arrived at the house after collecting Ana from Heathrow to find a message on my telephone answering machine asking me to ring Surrey police urgently.

I called the number given, with no inkling of what the police could possibly want to talk to me about, and found myself once again near to collapse, my mind swimming, as I listened to a stranger's voice giving me the most dreadful news. My stepson, Guy Robinson, had been found dead in his car, I was told. The sympathetic officer on the other end of the line added that a member of the family would be required to visit Guildford Hospital to make a formal identification.

Hearing this myself was awful enough – I had been closely involved in Guy's upbringing since he was a boy and had come to love him as I would my own son – but having to break the news to Jill was much, much worse, by far the most difficult and painful thing I have ever had to do. She was, of course, inconsolable and will never really get over the loss of her only child. No amount of time can heal that sort of grief.

Neither of us will ever quite be able to understand what it was that led Guy to decide that life was no longer worth living. There had certainly been no indication in the months beforehand that anything was desperately wrong. And, anyway, he had never been a particularly depressive type. If anything, he tended to be quite aggressively self-willed and headstrong and a bit like me insofar as he always insisted on doing things his way or no way at all. This inevitably led to personality clashes during those periods when he came to work for me, in between spells as a PR with Rothmans and with various agencies, and we locked horns on several occasions. Ironically, it was only towards the end that our relationship started to blossom and we became really good mates.

By then, he had taken on the job of running Minilite, specialists in rally car wheels and one of the oldest-established and most famous names in motorsport. The company had been on the verge of going under after the previous owner, David Lee, suffered a stroke and when Guy heard that David was anxious to find a buyer who would keep the name going, he went out and raised the £100,000 needed to take it over and get it up and running again.

He had then experienced a few problems to do with the trademark and also some minor financial difficulties, but nothing too serious, as I discovered when, as his executor, I started going through his affairs in detail. Apart from that, his marriage to Joanna, the mother of his son, Jamie, had ended in divorce and a subsequent relationship wasn't progressing quite as smoothly as he would have liked.

Which of these factors, if any, finally pushed him over the edge is something we shall never know for sure. The only solace we have is provided by Jamie, a wonderfully bright and very determined teenager who is never happier than when he is under the bonnet of one of our cars with the Team mechanics and who is already bent on being a rally driver himself one day.

Given the terrible troubles by which we were beset, it is perhaps hardly surprising that the second half of 1997 remains something of a blank in my mind as far as any actual rallying is concerned. The records show that Jimmy McRae won the Historic Scottish for us again, with Mike Hibbert lying 2nd at one stage and promising to make it a one-two for Historic Motorsport until he had problems with an oil filter.

Once again, the old-timer had impressed his co-driver, this time David Nicholson, with his evergreen skills. David had been worried in practice that Mike seemed a bit too slow, perhaps showing his age, but once the timekeeper signalled the start of the rally it was if Dr Jekyll had turned in an instant into Mr Hyde as they exploded off the starting ramp. "I suddenly realised I had better get my own act together," recalls David.

In an endeavour to brighten up our lives a little and to put the previous six months behind us, Jill and I spent the New Year holidays in San Francisco and Los Angeles, along with Ana and her children - Rita, Mario and Pablo. By now we had become close family friends, Jill and I acting as guardians to the two boys while they were being educated in England at Stoneyhurst College in Lancashire.

Sadly, we had no sooner returned home after the holiday than gloom descended yet again with the news that Roger Clark, Britain's best ever rally driver and a close friend for many years, had died suddenly. I was once more plunged into despair, convinced that with my friends and family dying all around me – Jill had also lost her mother in 1997 – it must be my turn soon.

The first real ray of hope for months came when Ana called me in early 1998, asking if I might be able to lend her an historic car for the Monte Carlo Challenge. Our break in California had obviously had some effect. She told me that, having had time to think things through, she had come to the conclusion that at just forty-five and with her children largely off her hands, she could not spend the rest of her life sitting at home, grieving. We both agreed that this was the last thing Ignacio would have wanted.

The only suitable car that I had available at the time was the Volvo PV that Jill had previously driven. I had this prepared for Ana and then Jill and I drove it down to Biarritz, one of that year's starting points. As only six cars were starting from there, I found myself being roped in by the organisers to man the time control as well.

Happily, it all went very well. With Ignacio's close friend Jose Fermin Armendariz as her driver, Ana thoroughly enjoyed the event and when she got to Monte Carlo she was re-united for the first time since Ignacio's death with many of their rallying mates. The social scene among the rally crowd in Monte Carlo is famously lively and Ana had a marvellous time, going out on the town and relaxing properly for the first time in months. On her last night there she sat down with us in the hotel and started talking seriously about getting back into rallying on a regular basis.

Having decided that she would like to start off with a crack at the Shield of Africa, another Transworld Events marathon to be run in the September of that year, it was then a matter of trying to find the right driver for her. After some thought, Jill came up with the suggestion of Mike Corns.

An experienced Historic driver in his fifties, easy-going and single, with no ex-wives to cause problems, Jill reckoned he might fit the bill perfectly. On being approached, Mike was all in favour, but sensibly suggested that he and Ana should try a couple of regular events so that they could get to know each other and make sure that they were compatible before embarking on a month-long marathon together. We all agreed that this was a good idea and duly selected the Circuit of Ireland, one of Ignacio's great favourites, and the Historic Welsh Rally, both of which went reasonably well.

In the meantime, we had been offered an exciting opportunity, quite out of the blue, when John Lloyd decided that he would like to drive a modern rally car in a World Championship event 'before he got too old' - his words, not mine! I asked him what car he wanted to drive and he replied that he would leave that up to me. Not having been actively involved in modern rallying for some six years I was a bit out of touch, so I rang two or three drivers, including Jimmy McRae, to ask what they would choose if they were going to drive a Group N car. They all came up with the same answer – a Mitsubishi.

I duly acquired a standard Mitsubishi Evo 4 and took it round to John's home so that he could have an initial test drive. He was absolutely delighted with it – as were my mechanics when it arrived in the workshop to be rebuilt as a rally car. Like me, they were thrilled to be back in the modern rally car business.

I wasn't quite so thrilled when John announced that he wanted to make his World Championship debut in the Safari. As I've already mentioned, this has never been my favourite event, largely because it is so hard on the cars, which routinely end up fit for little else but the breaker's yard. However, there were obvious reasons why John should have picked it. Apart from the sentimental attachment arising from his family connections both with Africa and with the event itself, he had already established a very impressive track record in the Historic section of the Safari over the previous three years. He had come 2nd in 1995 before then winning it the following year in a Peugeot 504, in which he shared the driving with 1984 East African Rally Champion David Horsey. In 1997, with Pauline Gullick as his co-driver, he had been very unlucky to get bogged down in deep sand in our Mark I Escort while lying 2nd.

He was again unfortunate in the Mitsubishi, being forced to retire when the rear suspension broke twice on the first day and we simply ran out of spares. This was the result of a design fault, for which the manufacturer apologised profusely. Thankfully, despite this disappointment, John's first taste of modern car rallying left him well and truly addicted and hungry for more.

In the meantime, it was back to Historic for the 1998 Shield of Africa. For this he was re-united with David Horsey in an Escort RS 1600, with Ana and Mike Corns in an identical car. This event, although marred by a fatality on the first day, was one of the most beautifully spectacular rallies I have ever been associated with.

Starting in Cape Town, the wonderfully scenic route took us first to Zimbabwe – where John and I took advantage of a two-day rest halt to enjoy a spectacular helicopter flight over the Victoria Falls – and then on through Botswana and back into South Africa, down past the Kruger National Park and all the way along the Garden Route to Cape Town. I remember the mechanics saying to me on the run-in to the final control: "We could have done with another week of this."

We would have enjoyed it even more had John not unfortunately had a monumental accident at a point when he was only seconds off the lead with what we felt was a very good chance of winning. Pressing perhaps a fraction too hard, he went into a corner flat out, lost control and spun into a tree. The fact that he walked away with nothing more serious than a cracked rib was, I like to think, testimony to the strength we build into our cars. Ana and Mike, meanwhile, drove very steadily to finish 5th overall.

The other highlights of our year included a third consecutive Historic Scottish Rally victory for Jimmy McRae and a further solid performance by Mike Corns and Ana in the 1000 Lakes.

Elsewhere, 1998 saw the end of an era when the Ford Escort finally went out of production on the 30th anniversary of its introduction. Ford decided to mark this historic occasion with a lavish black tie party to which they invited all those who had been associated in any meaningful way over that period with what is generally acknowledged as one of the most successful road and rally marques of all time. Given my contribution to their British and World Championship triumphs of 1980 and

1981 I was therefore extremely hurt and disappointed to find that I had somehow been missed off the guest list.

Many of those who did attend were shocked by my absence and I know for sure that David Richards and Ari Vatanen complained bitterly to Ford, who later offered their apologies, blaming the oversight on "an administrative error". To this day I do not know what really happened but it does seem odd that they should have forgotten who had won the Drivers' World Championship for them nearly twenty years earlier – a feat that, at the time of writing, Ford, with all the resources at their command, have never managed to repeat.

Very shortly after this, Ana and I had a good excuse for some celebrations of our own when, on December 9, 1998 we threw a small party at Historic Motorsport's new Rutherford Way premises to mark the official opening of the private rally car museum that Ana had had built in Ignacio's memory and which features many rally cars from his collection. At the time of his death, this amounted to nearly one hundred classic cars of all kinds, including around twenty of his favourite Mercedes.

The museum currently features thirty cars, altogether worth more than £3 million. Starting with a Mini driven by Timo Mäkinen in 1963, they span forty years of rally history and while many of them have famous connections, some are famous in their own right. For instance, the Audi Quattro, registration number LYV 4X, that we prepared for Hannu Mikkola in the early eighties is probably the most photographed Quattro of them all, featured in just about every magazine, book and video touching on the Group B era.

Looking around the museum, visitors often ask which car I would rescue first if the building were burning down and this is the one I always pick out. It was the first car we ever prepared for Audi, after moving from Ford in 1982, and therefore represents another important landmark in my career. I am enormously proud to have been involved right from the very start with all the excitement of that fabulous four-wheel-drive, turbo-charged Group B era and the trail-blazing technology that went with it. Apart from that, we won a lot of events in that car. When Hannu left Audi it passed into private hands and was then sold on again before we eventually bought it back and spent five years restoring it.

Among several other Quattros that we have on display is an S1 with the chassis number 001, the first of only twenty ever made. We also have the A2 Quattro that Stig Blomqvist drove to victory in the 1983 RAC and a road-going Sport Quattro in which Jill was once pulled over by the police after clocking 125 mph on the motorway. She insisted that it was perfectly safe – it was late at night and there was nothing else on the road at the time – and the officers concerned were so surprised when she explained that she had only put her foot down for a moment or two ("just testing", as it were!) that they let her off with a caution.

We have another A1 Quattro that I found behind a pile of cardboard boxes in the workshops of Volkswagen Racing in South Africa. When I checked it out, I discovered, to my surprise, that it was actually the Works car that had been driven by South African Champion Sarel van der Merve. I managed to buy it for a nominal price and we are currently restoring it at a cost of around £40,000.

It was in South Africa, once again, that I came across two full-blown Quattro A4 Super Touring Team circuit cars that I duly acquired, complete with fourteen crates of spares. We are hoping to race them it one day if we can just find a category that will accept them.

Every car in the museum has an interesting story attached to it. There is the Talbot Sunbeam Lotus in which Henri Toivonen won the RAC in 1980, an awesome Lancia Stratos similar to that driven by Bjorn Waldegard in the mid-seventies and the even more thunderously powerful Lancia 037 in which Markku Alen won the San Remo and which Hannu, much to his embarrassment, then managed to crash at Silverstone while taking part in a special celebrity event we staged there in 2001.

And, of course, there are examples of the Escorts and Lotus Cortinas that we have rallied so successfully over the years.

There are two strikingly sleek-looking Renault Alpines, one a circuit-racing model with flared wheel arches and the other a rally car that Ignacio gifted to Jill in his will; a 1960s Skoda that has competed in every marathon up to and including the Panama-Alaska and the 2000 London-Sydney; the RS 200 that became the last Group B car ever to be entered in an event by Ford when they ran it in the 1986 RAC; and the Volvo PV 544 that I found long abandoned, but perfectly preserved, under an apple tree in an overgrown orchard in California and on which we subsequently carried out one of our best restoration projects.

As well as the cars, the museum also features various other items of historical interest such as photographs, videos, documentary records and memorabilia, including a pair of Roger Clark's overalls and the helmet that Luis Moya famously hurled through the back window of his car in frustration, both of which items Ana bought in charity auctions

For various administrative and security reasons we have not so far been able to open the museum to the general public and admission has to be by appointment only, mostly for groups of enthusiasts organised by motor clubs and other interested bodies. Meanwhile, we are currently looking at ways of expanding it and making it more widely accessible to the growing army of rally fans for whom it provides a colourful living history of our sport.

THE GODFATHER

The start of the New Year saw the usual invasion from Canada and the USA for the Historic Monte Carlo rally. This time they included, most notably, Tom Jones and Ralph Beckman in a Lotus Cortina. Belfast-born Tom had been a Works driver for BMC and for Ford in Canada in the mid sixties and had lost none of his original flair while Ralph, his regular co-driver, was a real 'scientist', whose meticulous attention to detail and skill over regularity sections was almost beyond belief. Even in those rallies that they didn't finish, they were never outside the Top Three at the point when they were forced to retire.

John Lloyd, meanwhile, had decided that he needed to improve his gravel-driving skills and asked me to arrange some private tuition with the very talented David Higgins at his Forest Experience Driving School in Carno Forest. Emerging with his confidence boosted sky-high, John then went straight out and rolled his Mitsubishi Evolution 4 down the side of a Yorkshire mountain in the Riponian Rally, having gone into a hairpin a little too ambitiously. However, the extra training was seen to have paid off handsomely when he then achieved a very satisfactory 2nd place overall in the Historic Circuit of Ireland, followed by good results in the Ypres and Manx events.

Mention of Ypres brings to mind the occasion a few years before this when David Richards very kindly offered to fly me over in his helicopter. On the way back I then found myself inadvertently involved in some competitive co-driving of a rather unexpected kind. What happened was that before crossing the Channel we had to drop in at Calais to complete some customs formalities and our take-off was then delayed by fog.

When we did eventually get airborne again, David revealed that he was due to take part in the British Helicopter Trials in Northamptonshire that afternoon, and, given that there was not now time to go home first, wondered whether I would mind if we went straight to the Trials? I said that was fine by me and, almost before I knew it, David was doing all sorts of fancy manoeuvres over Castle Ashby while, at one point, I found myself dropping bags of sand from a height of about 100 feet onto a target below.

It was all rather jolly, but quite casual, and it wasn't until weeks later that I discovered David had actually won the whole competition. As I keep reminding him, I still haven't had my share of the winnings!

On a gloomier note, the rallying bereavements continued with the loss of Des O'Dell, the famously ebullient team manager for Talbot who had chased me around the world back in 1981 as we battled it out for the World Championship. The competition was intense, especially when it became clear that it was going to go right down to the wire, but it was played out in the most fantastic spirit. This was perhaps best illustrated during the famous incident in 1980 when Ari and Hannu crashed out of the Rally of Portugal in such spectacular fashion, their cars landing on top of each other.

Henri Toivenen's Talbot suffered a broken axle on the same special stage and as Des and I waited together for all the other cars to clear the stage before being allowed to go in and sort things out, Des asked me if I would consider doing him a big favour by getting my mechanics to fix Henri's axle for him. As Des pointed out, both my cars were now out of it so we wouldn't be going anywhere. At the same time, if he had to wait around with his service van to go and rescue Henri he would never be able to catch up with his surviving car.

I was only too happy to oblige. Like me, Des was representing a manufacturer but with a small, low-budget Team, so we had a lot in common. We were going head-to-head out on the road but we regularly got together in the service areas for a chat, commiserating about shared problems and generally putting the world to rights. It was the same with the mechanics. Everybody was out to win, but there was always time for a few drinks together at the end of the day. Sadly, that sort of camaraderie no longer seems to exist today, with everybody apparently trying to trip each other up and catch each other out with technicalities.

At around the same time that Des died we also lost the superb rally technician Robin Vokins. Robin had a long and distinguished career with BMC before later moving to Ford, where he remained until his untimely death following an operation.

There was better news in 1999 with the announcement that we were once again going to be teaming up with Hannu Mikkola and Ford for another marathon. This time it was the 2000 London-Sydney and what added an extra dimension of interest was Hannu's insistence that his co-driver for the event should be his eldest son, Juha.

As Juha's godfather, I had obviously followed the young man's progress very closely from the moment I went over to Helsinki for his christening, which was conducted in English rather than Finnish largely for my benefit. I was also present for his confirmation and for his formal graduation from the International College in Helsinki, a ceremony presided over by the British Ambassador and followed by a party at the Mikkola's waterside home on the outskirts of the capital.

Unlike his younger brother, Vesa, Juha had never shown any great desire to follow in his father's footsteps as a rally driver, but nevertheless jumped at the opportunity to spend some real quality time with his dad while at the same time enjoying the adventure of a lifetime. In characteristic fashion, he went away and prepared himself so thoroughly that, despite having had no previous experience, he went on to do a brilliant job, making virtually no mistakes at all during a gruelling and highly demanding month-long event that involved forty or fifty special stages along the 10,000-mile route.

My own preparations for the event included the usual arrangements for the pre-positioning of spare parts, wheels and tyres at intervals along the route and also the setting up of strategic command centres in friends' offices in Turkey and Malaysia from where I could mastermind our whole operation

We were looking after five cars altogether. As well as Hannu and Juha, for whom we had rebuilt the 1995 London-Mexico Escort H1 FEV, loaned to us by Ford, we had also entered Ana and Mike Corns, plus a third Escort that was to be driven by mechanics Gareth Williams and John O'Connor, who had recently returned to the fold after a three-year spell in Paraguay. Fully laden with a copious supply of spare parts and tools, the latter, I have to admit, was effectively a chase car. This was well within the regulations, although one or two of our rivals did consider it to be a little over the top.

In addition to the three Escorts there were also two Cortinas, one of which we prepared for private client Anthony Ward while the other, driven by Chris Underwood, was a charity entry sponsored by Unilever. This was due to be auctioned afterwards, with the proceeds going to the Great Ormond Street Hospital for Children.

It soon became clear that Hannu, Juha and the Escort were by far the quickest combination in the rally , but, frustratingly, they had absolutely no luck at all. They were doing very nicely until they went off the road in Thailand, but soon fought their way back into the lead, establishing a pattern that continued from then on. Time and again they would run into a problem that would drop them back to 5th or 6th, after which they would claw their way back only for something else untoward to happen.

Arriving in Australia, they were particularly unlucky to be penalised in freak circumstances. A backpacking Kiwi mechanic, who had briefly worked for us in Daventry in the past, happened to be visiting Darwin when the rally passed through and dropped in to say hello at the workshop where the Escort was being serviced. The Clerk of the Course looked in while he was there and immediately announced that Hannu was guilty of illegal servicing. Despite protests and appeals, a penalty was applied and he once again lost the lead that he had built up.

Victory might still have been possible given Hannu's speed and experience, but our hopes were finally dashed four or five days out from Sydney when the electrics drowned during a fairly routine river crossing. It took thirty minutes to re-start the car and we would probably have retired then and there had it not been for the fact that Juha was determined to record an official finish. Driving purely for the fun of it, Hannu then set a whole string of fastest times, just to remind everyone who was the boss.

While all this was going on, Ana and Mike Corns had been in a monumental accident, totally destroying their Escort. They had already had a couple of near misses before Mike, driving very fast, lost control on a corner and went off the road, rolling the car six or seven times in spectacular fashion.

Ana was taken to hospital but, fortunately, was found to have suffered only minor whiplash injuries. I breathed a sigh of relief, thankful that once again an Escort prepared by us had proved strong enough to protect the occupants in the most extreme circumstances, underlining once again the value of the extra time and money we invest in our roll cages and safety equipment.

This incident signalled the end of Ana's driving partnership with Mike Corns. In the end, Mike, although a very charming character, didn't always handle Ana's occasionally fiery Latin temperament quite as well as he might have done, on top of which he tended to be a little too laid-back at times in his general approach. Another big guy, who must have tipped the scales at about twenty stone, he never bothered too much about getting himself into shape and it sometimes appeared that the most important thing to him about any rally was the dinner reservation. He certainly seemed to know all the best restaurants in every rally location.

Not that this can't be a very useful attribute on the Historic circuit, where the social aspect is often quite an important part of the package for some of the competitors, especially on the long distance events. However, as I was very soon to discover, Ana had suddenly become altogether more ambitious and was keen to raise her game.

In the meantime, I had passed a significant landmark earlier in the year with the celebration of my 60th birthday. I had arranged a small private lunch party for friends and family at the Butcher's Arms, but just before we were due to leave for the restaurant I was asked if I would like to open some of the presents that had begun to pile up in considerable quantities. One of them, I was then told, was waiting for me outside the front door and when I went out to have a look I was completely stunned to find a brand new S-Type Jaguar, complete with the personalised registration V60 DLS, sitting in the drive with an array of coloured balloons floating above it.

I make no absolutely no apologies for the fact that for the next half an hour or so I was a gibbering wreck, tearful and emotional. Later, when I had eventually pulled myself together, Jill explained that she had almost given up hope of getting the car in time for my birthday because there was such a long waiting list for delivery. It was only at the very last moment that she had managed to jump the queue thanks to help from an unexpected quarter.

We might have reckoned we had some pretty good contacts in the motor industry, but none of them had been able to pull any strings simply because there was so much demand for the popular new model. At the Butcher's Arms, however, Lino has been serving top Jaguar executives on a regular basis ever since the days of Sir William Lyons and 'Lofty' England and when he heard that Jill was having problems he simply picked up the phone and within twenty-four hours the car, in my favourite colour, was on its way. They say that the way to a man's heart is through his stomach and the same obviously goes for motor company executives.

It was after we had arrived at the restaurant, and as Lino was serving us with a glass of champagne, that Jill told me this story and I was still chuckling over it when I felt a tap on my shoulder and a very familiar voice said: "Happy birthday, bugger." There is only one person in the world who routinely greets me with that particular endearment so, before I even turned round, I knew who it was. Hannu Mikkola had flown over from Finland the previous day, staying overnight with David and Karen Richards. The three of them then made their surprise entrance along with the lovely Michele Mouton.

Needless to say, I had to put up with a fair amount of mickey taking during the day's proceedings, much of it orchestrated by my younger brother Stuart. Apart from a faded photo of me as a choirboy that he had dug out from some old family album and had then had blown up into a lifesize cardboard cut-out, a great deal of merriment was prompted by his cod review of a car identified as the Model DS.

"Launched at the beginning of World War II, this unique 1940 classic has mellowed magnificently. Widely admired for its uncomplicated nature and timeless good looks – though built for comfort rather than speed – the Model DS has travelled from 0-60 with style and panache, powered solely by fine food and fine wine. Despite thousands of pounds spent on renovation over recent years the bodywork now shows advanced signs of deterioration and it is unlikely that the concourse condition of earlier years will ever be recovered. In contrast, the power unit is as good today as it has always been and the Model DS has circumvented the globe on many occasions, albeit protectively shrouded in Business Class. Outdated, outmoded and oblivious to modern technology, it is hoped that the Model DS will be around for many years to come." Thanks, Stuart.

The party went on all day and well into the night and, not

surprisingly, I was in no fit state to go into the office the following morning. When I did eventually make an appearance I was brought back down to earth with a bang. Despite all the congratulations that were still ringing in my ears I was aware that I was not particularly popular with my clients at that moment, the year's programme having got off to a less than auspicious start. The engine of Ana and Carl Bailey's Escort had blown itself to pieces on Philip Young's Monte Carlo Challenge while Tom Jones and Ralph Beckman had suffered a similar failure with their Lotus Cortina on the AC Monaco Monte Historic Rally.

When you have travelled half way around the world and have spent a small fortune to take part in a rally it is very disappointing to find yourself going home when the event is only a few hours old. And when mechanical failure is to blame rather than driver error, the finger of suspicion inevitably swings round to point at the people responsible for preparing the car. However, as I took stock of my career at this sixty-year milestone, any vague thoughts I may have entertained about maybe taking things a bit easier in the near future were quickly banished during the course of that year's 1000 Lakes.

Ana had invited Roger Clark's younger son, Oliver, to drive the event with her in a Mitsubishi Evo 4, which he promptly proceeded to park in the trees on the first day. Like his elder brother, Matthew, who worked for me as a mechanic for a while and for whom I'd previously organised a couple of drives in a Works Sierra Cosworth - only to watch him crash out on both occasions - Oliver had shown some early promise, winning one or two national events. But neither of them had quite inherited a full set of rallying genes from his father.

It is always hard for a son to follow in a famous father's footsteps, especially in the sporting arena. As far as rallying is concerned, Colin McRae is the obvious exception that proves the rule. And as mentioned earlier, although Hannu's elder son, Juha, has never really been that interested, his youngest, Vesa, is very keen and, with Hannu's cautious encouragement, has already taken the first steps towards making a career as a driver.

I watched Vesa going through his paces at a rally school in Finland and you could see definite signs that he might be a chip off the old block. He then went on to do well enough in one of the popular one-make series in Finland for Hannu to decide that he was ready to move up a gear and, with this in mind, he bought one of our Mitsubishis and gave it to him.

It was while we were in Jyväskylä for the 1000 Lakes that Ana invited me to a meeting with herself and former World Champion Stig Blomqvist at which, quite out of the blue, she sprung the surprise announcement that they had decided they would like to drive some World Championship events together with a Group N car in 2001 and wanted me to do it with them.

It turned out that they had hatched this plan after meeting during the London-Sydney, which Stig had eventually gone on to win in a Ford Capri Pirana. I was staggered. How many events were they thinking of doing, I asked? About eight, they replied. What's more, they added that they wanted a completely new, full-blown Team.

And so it was that exactly twenty years after my last challenge for the World Rally Championship I quite unexpectedly found myself back in the thick of it with a new Team, a good product, a former World Champion and a very decent budget. To signal my return and to separate the new venture from our Historic activities, I even resurrected David Sutton (Cars) Ltd, the old original company that had been sitting on the shelf ever since we switched from Ford to Audi back in 1982.

Fortunately, the initial discussion with Ana and Stig took place in August and the first event of the new season, the Swedish Rally, was not until the following February, so I had a bit of time in which to get everything set up. Even so, it was pretty tight, given that we were starting from scratch and needed to find cars, practice cars, trucks, trailers, motor homes, mechanics – the lot.

I have to admit that at this stage I was rather apprehensive.

Never in my wildest dreams had I ever imagined that I would be given the opportunity to get involved again in World Championship rallying at the highest level. Was I too old? Could I still do it? These were the kind of thoughts that inevitably flashed through my mind. Things had changed dramatically in the time that I had been away – new companies, new people and new cars – and I was only too well aware of the danger that I could end up making a fool of myself if I was not very careful. I therefore decided to keep a low profile at first while I felt my way back in, concentrating all my attention on making sure that the Team looked right, that the cars were properly set up and that we were seen to be doing a solid professional job.

We all had something to prove, not least Stig. At 55, he was almost as old as me, well past his sell-by date in modern rally driving terms, and there were a few raised eyebrows from those in the sport who felt that maybe Ana should have spent her money on giving a young driver a break. That, however, was never really an option. Quite understandably, one of the main attractions of the whole deal for Ana was the opportunity to team up with a former World Champion, especially one as enduringly popular as Stig, who still attracts crowds of adoring fans wherever he goes.

Apart from that, there was the safety angle to be considered. With a younger, less experienced driver there was always a much greater risk that Ana would finish upside down on the roof – as she did with Oliver Clark in Finland. At her age - and as the mother of three children, albeit grown-up ones – that had to be a consideration. The accident with Mike Corns during the London-Sydney had concentrated her mind in this respect. With Stig, who rarely puts so much as a scratch on the car, she feels very safe and very comfortable

We weren't expecting any miracles from him. He certainly wasn't the driver he had been when we won the British Championship together in 1983. Even so, given his experience and a dependable car, I thought we had the potential to do very well in Group N. In fact, if he could live up to his reputation for reliability and consistently finish somewhere among the Top Five, there was a mathematical possibility that we could win the Championship.

Safe and sensible as his driving might be, Stig soon made it very clear that he had lost none of his ambition or his fiercely competitive urge. One thing that we had all agreed upon at that inaugural meeting in Finland was that, first and foremost, our involvement should be an enjoyable experience, without any unnecessary pressure. Stig, however, seemed to have forgotten all about that even before the first event of the season in Sweden, insisting on a long and expensive test session with special gear boxes, special wheels, and all manner of other special requirements – none of which had been included in the budget. Suddenly, he had started to behave like a Works World Champion again.

Partly out of well-meaning but misplaced patriotism and partly, I suspect, out of desire to provide jobs for the boys, he also demanded that the team should be as Swedish as possible. We had to have a Swedish engine management system, Swedish suspension, Swedish brake pads, Swedish-made clothing and even some Swedish staff. We reluctantly went along with this in the early days largely to keep Stig happy, but, quite frankly, a lot of the Swedish gear was absolute rubbish and when the brake pads were found to be disintegrating into powder it gave me the welcome excuse to blow the whistle and order a change of suppliers.

This all created a little bit of an atmosphere at first, but we nevertheless managed to get off to a very reasonable start. I had used the previous November's Network Q Rally as a shakedown event for the team and although we had to retire with rear suspension failure I felt that we could well have achieved a very different result if Stig had changed a punctured tyre instead of trying to drive on through a very rutted stage - the same section, incidentally, on which Colin McRae had rolled. But in Sweden he more than made up for this, finishing 3rd in Group N.

We had deliberately omitted Monte Carlo from our programme because we felt that the event was a bit of a tyre lottery and Stig is perhaps not best remembered for his performances on tarmac. Our next outing was in the Portuguese Rally. We had expected to do well here in what, traditionally, had always been the sort of rough, tough gravel event in which you needed a bucketful of experience, something that Stig obviously had in abundance. It turned out, instead, to be a disaster. We arrived to find that the roads were not worthy of a World Championship event – the locals told us that it had been raining there almost continuously for six months - and it has since been removed from the Championship roster. We were forced to retire after the gearbox failed on a special stage, but, fortunately for us, the two leading Group N cars were both excluded because of a technical infringement, so we were hopeful that a good result in Spain the following month might put us right back on track.

Stig and I were still not seeing entirely eye-to-eye at this stage, the main bone of contention during this particular event being a difference of opinion about fuel levels. The simple and obvious truth is that if you cut it too fine there is always the danger that your challenge could fizzle out in the most embarrassing circumstances. Better, in my view, to err on the side of caution. This dispute rumbled on and on, with Stig endlessly critical of the weight of the car resulting from what he considered to be an excess of fuel. He also whinged on about a number of other items, nagging at me constantly while at the same time insisting that everyone else's Group N cars were illegal.

The reality, I had begun to suspect, was that he was being out-driven by some very fast youngsters and was having a problem coming to terms with this. I must hold up my hands at this point and admit that I myself, having my first dabble in Group N after such a long time away from the World Championship, had badly underestimated the standard of the opposition, not realising how quick some of these guys were going to be.

We just about managed to hang in there in Spain, finishing in 3rd place thanks largely to the failure of others, but then suffered three consecutive retirements in Argentina, Cyprus and Greece. Our failure in Argentina was particularly frustrating. Like Portugal, this was another demanding gravel event that seemed tailor-made for Stig, who had won there in the past, and, indeed, we were doing quite well until the engine blew up.

Clearly, our Championship was going nowhere and the only straw I could grasp at was that the pattern was rather similar to 1981, when Ari Vatanen also drew a blank in Portugal and Argentina, having confidently expected to come away with a bagful of points. The parallel was then further extended when Ana very generously decided that we might be able to pick up a few extra points by adding the Safari Rally in Kenya to our programme, just as Rothmans had done by sending us to the Ivory Coast event when our 1981 World Championship challenge was faltering.

We put a huge amount of effort into the Safari, building a brand new car to Safari specifications, shipping over a huge range of spare parts and taking out no less than twelve mechanics. After all that, our participation ended prematurely yet again when, on the second day, the electric fan mounting broke and forced its way into the radiator. We had now suffered five retirements in seven events.

To add to our disappointment, John Lloyd, in a second car, had to retire with exactly the same problem. Whilst most of our effort was going into the World Championship, we had not lost sight of our responsibilities to the clients of Historic Motorsport who had been enjoying considerable success. John had started his African Rally Championship programme with a fine 2nd overall in Namibia and was about to repeat that result in South Africa until a freak accident sent the car off the road.

We had also been asked to look after the official Peugeot entry in the World Cup Rally with Barbara Armstrong and Alison

Marlow and they rewarded us with a superb 2nd place. After being featured in an extensive promotional tour for Peugeot the car now resides in our museum.

At the same time, I wanted to support Francis Tuthill's newly conceived Evo Africa Rally. John Lloyd very generously loaned us his Escort RS 1600, which was driven by South African rallying legend Sarel Van der Merwe with, as his co-driver, Stuart Pegg, winner of the 1976 RAC with Roger Clark. Sarel, as usual, was leading by a considerable distance when he crashed off the road and totally destroyed John's car, which I have since replaced.

Meanwhile, our Group N fortunes improved dramatically over the last four events of our programme with 4th place finishes in New Zealand and San Remo, 7th in Australia and 5th in the RAC. This very satisfactory run-in lifted us to 5th overall in both the Championship and the FIA Teams Cup but, although this was a much better result than had at one time seemed likely, it was still a long way from what I had confidently expected when we set out. That, of course, was before I had had a chance to size up the opposition. I was particularly impressed by the performance of the eventual winner, a young Argentinian named Gabriel Pozzo who seemed to me to be blessed with real star quality.

In fretting over what I considered to be our own rather disappointing performance I was probably as guilty as Stig had been of forgetting that we had gone into it with the specific aim of having fun and not putting ourselves under pressure to win at all costs. The important thing was that Ana seemed to have enjoyed herself – so much so that even before the season ended on a relatively high note she had already decided that she wanted to go one step further.

Once again I found myself listening in amazement when she called me to a meeting and calmly announced that she wanted me to see if I could set her and Stig up with a drive in a full-blown World Rally Car.

CZECH MATES

Those wheel really had now come full circle. As a result of being involved in Group N rather than just Historic rallying Ana had started to mix with a slightly different crowd that included a lot of world-class drivers and co-drivers and, as a result, she had become enthused with the idea of testing herself at the very highest level in a World Rally car. To start with, she had decided that she would like to rent a drive in the 1000 Lakes.

That is easier said than done. I went first to Martin Whitaker at Ford to ask what it would cost to run Stig and Ana as part of their Team but, to this day, he has not even accorded me the courtesy of a reply; the Subaru price was outrageous; and Mitsubishi were simply too committed. In the end it was an old pal of mine at Skoda who came up trumps and agreed to run an extra car in Finland.

I went along to hold Ana's hand and watched as she and Stig turned in a creditable performance that left her eager for more. Afterwards we sat down with the Skoda bosses and hammered out a deal whereby they agreed to field a third a car for a programme of twelve events in the 2002 season, to be divided equally between Stig and Ana and a promising young Czech driver called Roman Kresta. This arrangement suited everybody very well, helping Skoda to finance Kresta and enabling us to negotiate a very reasonable price for Stig and Ana, who would officially be part of the Skoda team but under our management.

At the same time, Ana wanted to hang on to the Mitsubishi Group N team that she sponsors partly through her family's vineyard, Bodega Otazu, and instructed me to look round for a young driver we could help. The man we eventually picked was

Martin Rowe. Martin had won the British Championship the year before and, although he is never quite going to be another Colin McRae or Richard Burns, he is a very talented driver and a good team player, someone who can always be relied upon to give you a good result, unless the car breaks. On top of that, he is an extremely nice guy, easy to work with and a pleasure to have around. With Chris Wood as his co-driver, Martin was duly contracted to do six events for us in the new Mitsubishi Evo 6.

While all this was being put in place, I had an unexpected approach from Martin Christie, Gabriel Pozzo's manager, with what I instantly regarded as a very exciting proposition. Armed with the promise of a substantial budget, Martin was looking for a World Rally Car berth for Pozzo for the 2002 season and had come to me in search of a deal.

I have always been more than happy to do whatever I can to give promising young drivers a leg up, partly out of the self-interested hope that I might one day discover a future World Champion. As it happened, I had already been keeping a very close eye on Pozzo's progress during the previous season as he came from nowhere to take the Group N Championship. Watching him in action, in a Mitsubishi that he was driving for an Italian team, I had quickly formed the opinion that this country boy from Argentina was the best 22-year-old prospect I had ever seen.

I was well aware that I was not the first person Martin had approached. He had already talked to all the major Works teams, including Ford, Mitsubishi and Subaru, but the sponsorship that he was able to bring to the table from Argentina was not enough to buy a seat in one of their Factory cars. However, from the dealings I had already had with Skoda, I was confident that I would be able to sort out some kind of arrangement with them.

Sure enough, they were very receptive and after several visits to their factory headquarters in Mlada Boleslav, near Prague, I managed to negotiate a deal whereby they agreed to lend us a

World Rally car for a year, plus a full kit of spares supplied on a sale-or-return basis. We would then operate as a satellite team, running the car for Skoda in up to ten events.

I also met representatives of Pozzo's sponsors, an Argentinian government agency set up specifically to promote the country's sports stars. Having already backed Pozzo's Group N season with the Italian team, they now agreed to put up a further $1 million to finance the Skoda deal, with the first payment due to be made on March 1st, 2002, just before our first event of the season, the Catalunya Rally.

As soon as the contracts were signed, we sent some of our engineers over to Mlada Boleslav to start work on preparing the car in the Skoda workshops. This was followed, in January, by testing in the Czech Republic and we then brought the car over to Daventry to make final checks and get everything ready for Catalunya.

In the meantime, the Argentinian economy had started to collapse. Because we were dealing with a bona fide Government agency we were confident that our deal was pretty much gilt-edged, but, when the first instalment of money failed to arrive in our bank account on time, alarm bells began to ring. March 1st fell on a Friday and we spent the weekend hoping against hope that it would prove to be a temporary hold-up or a typical South American bureaucratic hitch, only for Martin to call first thing on Monday with the dreaded news that, amid escalating political and financial chaos, the agency had been disbanded and that, sadly, there was going to be no money.

It was shades of 1992 all over again. Already committed to the extent of the £70,000 or so that we had already spent on getting the car ready, we were now left with two options. Either we could cut our losses straightaway and return the car and everything that went with it to Skoda or we could kick the programme off ourselves in the hope that the situation in Argentina would improve in the very near future, or that some sort of alternative deal could eventually be arranged.

I called Ana to ask whether she would be able to help out with a bit of extra sponsorship to tide us over. As I explained to her, I felt that we had to find a way of hanging in there, if only in the interests of our own credibility. Apart from that, I believed so strongly in Pozzo's potential at a time when everybody was looking out for new young drivers that I felt we had to try to hold onto him. After listening to all this, Ana kindly agreed to pay for the Catalunya entry.

What we now desperately needed was a good result. We didn't get it. Pozzo was doing very well given that it was his first-ever event in a World Rally car, but then, on the second day, the turbo charger caught fire and he was forced to retire. Skoda were very good about it and allowed us to re-build the fire-damaged car in their factory, free of charge.

The next scheduled event was the Cyprus Rally. This was funded at the last minute by a couple of private businessmen in Argentina who were anxious to keep their young fellow countryman's challenge going. On this occasion he did at least manage to finish - but only just. Everything on the car kept breaking and I think it would be fair to say that this was largely because the Czech way of doing things and the English way of doing things are not quite the same when it comes to rally engineering.

After Cyprus came Argentina, Gabriel's home event. Obviously, this was the big one as far as he was concerned, but we were still leading a hand-to-mouth existence and, as there was no sign at all of anyone else coming forward with an offer of funding, it was beginning to look as though we would have to scratch. At this point, in an act of tremendous kindness and generosity, Ana announced that she and Stig would stand down from what was one of their contracted events so that Pozzo could have their Factory car.

He duly rewarded us all by coming home in 9th place, with the crowd going absolutely wild around him. There was one point I will always remember when he was besieged in the motor home, unable to force his way through the fans to get to his car in the service area. This only served to convince me that we could be on a real roll with this young man and I decided to sign him to a two-year contract just to make sure that if I did succeed in getting him through the year and then into a top team, nobody else was going to steal him without at least having to pay a lot of money to buy us out.

I was soon congratulating myself on my shrewdness and foresight in this respect as Skoda almost immediately served notice on me to the effect that they wanted first option on him for the following year. We even went so far as to start talking about his programme and salary. At this stage I definitely thought I was in the £1 seats! We had invested £100,000 of our own money in Gabriel up until this point, but I now reckoned we would be getting it back with interest.

We therefore arrived in Greece for the Acropolis in buoyant mood, despite slight problems in preparing the car that Skoda had agreed to loan us for the event. The spec was old and we had had to spend a lot of time trying to get it right.

Even so, it seemed to be going well until Gabriel made a silly little mistake, more out of a lack of experience than anything else. There tends to be as much dust around on the Acropolis as there is on the Safaris and, having driven superbly during the final stage of the first day to catch the car in front, he suddenly found himself driving blind in its dust stream. He misjudged a corner as a result and slid quite gently off the road. The car was completely undamaged but, frustratingly, he couldn't get it back on the road and had to retire.

Disappointment turned to bitter despair a few days later when, without any warning whatsoever, a letter arrived from Skoda bluntly announcing that they had no further interest in Pozzo either for the that year or the next and adding that they would be grateful if we would kindly return the car and all the other equipment they had loaned to us as soon as possible.

This came as a bombshell that knocked us all sideways. I couldn't imagine what it was that had so suddenly dampened their enthusiasm for Gabriel, prompting such an unexpected U-turn, and all my efforts to find out more about their reasons drew a complete blank. They insisted that they had simply had second thoughts and there certainly seemed to be no hard feelings on their side. In the end, the only explanation I could think of was that, for political reasons, they had been put under pressure to promote a Czech driver.

Under the terms of my contract with Gabriel, I had until November 2002 to come up with an alternative drive for him at which point the option would run out and he would become a free agent. Unfortunately, I was unable to convince anybody else that he was going to be the next big thing and, sadly, I had to let him go. I still believe he could be a World Champion one day. Watch this space!

While all this was going on, I had begun to find myself becoming increasingly involved behind the scenes as an unofficial spokesman for the Group N team managers at a time when the organisation of our sport was starting to go through many far-reaching and occasionally controversial changes. And while I applaud most of the moves aimed at raising the profile of World Rally and establishing it as a serious popular rival to Formula 1, I and my colleagues in the lower divisions do have reservations about some aspects of the revolution that is now in full swing, brilliantly and energetically led by my old friend David Richards.

Like many people, including David himself, I have a great nostalgia for the sort of rallying with which we both grew up, with all the excitement of roadside servicing, chase cars and non-stop, no-holds-barred races through the night, from one end of a country to the other. At the same time, we all recognise that from both a practical and a safety point of view there is no place for that kind of thing on today's congested roads. It is actually astonishing to think that, until quite recently, we were still barrelling through villages and even small towns in places like Greece and Portugal, hurtling down High Streets and jumping bridges along routes lined with crowds of curious shoppers and innocent bystanders, while a handful of traffic cops held back the regular traffic and waved us through!

By comparison, modern rallies with their central service areas and special stages condensed into small areas are rather sanitised affairs. The Rally of Great Britain takes place in the Welsh forests, even the Safari Rally doesn't venture that far out of Nairobi these days and only the occasional classic marathons capture some of the old spirit. And yet, paradoxically, the World Rally Championship has never been more popular, has never before generated so much excitement among so many millions of fans worldwide. The simple reason for that, of course, is television.

Television coverage has changed the whole nature of rallying. It used to be almost entirely a participatory sport. Events were wholly geared around that fundamental understanding and were funded on the entry fee alone. There were very few spectators and if the national Press or the television cameras turned up it was purely incidental, any interest of that sort being confined almost exclusively to the Monte Carlo Rally. Nowadays it is driven almost entirely by the needs of television. I have no quarrel with that – it's the only way for any sport to go in our televisual age. And in this respect there can be no doubting that David Richards has done an absolutely fantastic job since he bought the exclusive rights to television coverage of the World Rally Championship from Bernie Ecclestone.

Helped by the enormous technological advances that can increasingly put cameras right at the very heart of the action, he has been able to generate a new dimension of excitement to the sport, attracting a whole new audience at a time when Formula 1 is becoming all too boringly predictable. Watching the same procession go round and round a series of Grand Prix circuits can't really compete with the sensation of being right there alongside the driver in a car that is going sideways into a corner at 100 mph or off the road and into the trees on its roof – especially if that car doesn't look that different to the one you drive to work in every day.

Further innovations now in the pipeline promise increasingly sophisticated interactive and virtual reality features that will eventually allow the armchair viewer to drive the special stages in competition with Colin McRae, Richard Burns and the rest. Meanwhile, we are told that Channel 4's extended coverage has already boosted UK viewing figures by well over 200% and that the introduction of live coverage is expected to raise the worldwide audience to around 150 million.

This is all very good commercial sense for the big factory teams, each of whom are now reckoned to be pouring an average £50 million a year into their campaigns. My concern is for the lesser teams and the privateers, who seem to me to be in danger not just of being left only with the crumbs from this table, but of not even being invited to the feast at all.

The problem arises out of the fact that the television cameras inevitably tend to focus only on the top teams and personalities, to the point where the audience might well conclude that there are only ever about ten cars in the rally, since those are the only ones you ever get to see. Unless, of course, there is a spectacular crash somewhere down the field.

When it comes to Group N and Super 1600, they hardly get a look in. Throughout the 2002 season we, as a professional team, did not have a single second of television time. Our sponsor happens to be one of Ana's own companies and she is reasonably relaxed about the lack of exposure, but a more aggressive sponsor would probably be crawling all over us wanting to know what they were getting in return for their investment.

I know that many of my fellow Group N managers, in particular, are extremely concerned not only about this but also about progressive rule changes over the last couple of years that have indirectly militated against the lesser teams with the smaller budgets. As a result, several have talked seriously about pulling out.

What worries us all is that in aiming to put itself on a par commercially with Formula 1, World Rally will end up with the same sort of problems that F1 is having to deal with now that all but the very richest teams have effectively been priced out of serious contention. In the face of flagging public interest, Bernie Ecclestone and the FIA are being forced to consider ever more artificial means of putting some excitement back into F1. It is that very lack of real excitement that is currently enabling World Rallying to put itself forward as a genuine alternative for motorsport enthusiasts in search of more thrilling fare. It would be a pity if we were to forget this point to the extent of falling foul of the same pitfalls.

With this debate going on in the background, we enjoyed mixed fortunes during the rest of the 2002 season. Ana decided after the Acropolis Rally that she had had enough of the WRC Championship with Skoda. I think she would probably agree that part of the reason for her waning enthusiasm was the fact that the rather different routine involved in being part of a Works team didn't really suit her. Having grown accustomed to calling the shots with us in the more relaxed situation where she was not only the most important client but also a major investor in the business, she found it hard to adjust to a situation where she was suddenly having to take orders from other people instead of giving them.

She returned to Group N for New Zealand, Australia and the RAC in the newly acquired Mitsubishi Evo 7. But before that, she and Stig, in an Escort, recorded their first victory together when they won the Historic Eiffel Rally in Germany, actually managing to beat Martin Rowe and Chris Wood, who were in another of our Escorts. Martin managed to get his own back in New Zealand, where a blinding drive secured him 2nd place, his best result of the campaign, but his 6th place in the Championship overall was nevertheless disappointing, largely the result of a design fault in the suspension arm which broke in exactly the same way in both Finland and Cyprus, leading to early retirement on both occasions.

John Lloyd was also out of luck in his Evo 4. In what must go down as one of the worst Safaris on record he looked as if he was heading for a Top Ten finish when a wire came off the alternator, while in the Equator Rally he was lying 2nd when he went off the road and was unable to re-start. He also suffered an early retirement on the RAC, so we weren't exactly flavour of the month with John, who had meanwhile been faring rather better in the Asia-Pacific Championship, finishing 5th overall in a car prepared by Neil Allport.

One way and another, it looked as though a year that had started so promisingly was going to end in anti-climax. As my 63rd birthday loomed, I was ready to contemplate the possibility once again of maybe slowing down and taking things a bit easier. No sooner had the thought started to cross my mind than I was approached with a proposition that was to give me yet another new lease of life at the top.

HERE WE GO AGAIN

I am very proud to have been closely associated with the first really big break of David Richards' spectacular career. And, of course, as Ari Vatanen's co-driver in our great Rothmans Ford teams of 1980 and 1981, he in turn played a vital part in helping me to reach the pinnacle of my own career as we won first the British and then the World Championship together.

Since then, of course, David has left us all far behind, going on to become the god of just about everything on four wheels, not only running the Subaru World Rally team and the BAR-Honda Formula 1 team simultaneously, but also finding time in between to mastermind the WRC's worldwide television operation as boss of ISC.

I often wonder how he manages to do all this when mere mortals like myself struggle to find enough hours in the day to run just a single private rally Team. The answer, I suspect, lies partly in the shrewd business acumen that he may well have started to develop in his days as an accountant, partly in his ability to surround himself with some very good people and partly in the sheer force of his own personality. I am reliably informed that when his car is outside in the car park the atmosphere inside the building is noticeably different. Apart from that, the thing that always struck me back in the Rothmans Ford days was his overall grasp of any situation and his ability to think very quickly on his feet.

I remember a particular occasion during the Brazilian Rally in 1981 when one of our service vans suddenly went down and, while the rest of us were deliberating over how best to compensate for this, he instantly worked out in his head exactly how we should move people around and re-organise our entire schedule. It was a small but impressive demonstration of the sort of management decision-making that I am sure is another major factor in his success.

Over the years I have remained in fairly close touch with 'D.R' – the initials by which he has generally been known in the business ever since the Rothmans Ford days, when he was one of five Davids in the Team and we needed a shorthand method of instant individual identification. However, I never really expected to have the opportunity of working with him again.

It was with the greatest pleasure and a keen sense of anticipation, therefore, that I was able to announce the new Group N deal for the 2003 season that has brought us back together after twenty-one years. The switch from Mitsubishi to Subaru – and from the Evo series to the exciting new Impreza WRX STI N9 – means that David Sutton Cars is effectively operating as a satellite Prodrive team for Group N. As part of this arrangement, the cars are being built at Prodrive's workshops by our own technicians, with all components being supplied by Prodrive along with technical support and advice.

Subaru had had their eye on us from the moment they decided to mount a serious challenge to Mitsubishi's domination of Group N, a category that has become increasingly popular with fans and enthusiasts alike, simply because the cars are seen to be both accessible and affordable. Up until the end of the 2001 season, Mitsubishi had been on a roll, recording no less than twenty-eight consecutive Group N victories and winning the Production Cup four years in a row. Subaru, meanwhile, had only dabbled rather half-heartedly in this section, concentrating their effort almost exclusively on the World Rally Championship.

Realising, rather belatedly, that Group N was worthy of much greater commitment, they produced a new car for the 2002 season and brought in Toshi Arai from the WRC team to drive it. At the same time, Prodrive tried informally to get us interested in switching from Mitsubishi, inviting us to go and see the car, to test drive it – even to borrow it for an event. At that stage we were quite happy to stay where we were. However, we watched Subaru's rapidly improving performance over the season with considerable interest and, when Prodrive then approached Ana yet again, I suggested that she should go along and see what sort of deal they had in mind.

The package they proposed was very attractive. As Ana said enthusiastically when she returned from the meeting: "For the first time since I've been rallying, somebody has actually offered to *give* me something!" As I later explained to Mitsubishi, in the four years that we had been with them we had spent more than £3 million rallying their cars and yet the most we'd ever had out of them was a free Team jacket from their merchandise range. There had certainly never been anything like the technical support and parts supply that Subaru were offering.

There were plenty of good, solid commercial reasons for Subaru's generosity. Under the rules governing Group N, manufacturers are not allowed to run their own Factory teams – they have to contract the job out to a private team. And, in the UK, we were the obvious choice. Not only did we have the facilities, the reputation and the track record – we were also the only private team in the UK that could afford a full World Championship programme. On top of that, we already had two very good drivers under contract in Stig Blomqvist and Martin Rowe.

From our point of view, of course, such a vote of confidence from a major manufacturer has provided a tremendous boost to morale, while moving on to a new product has revitalised the workforce. From the moment the deal was announced, everybody at Daventry was jumping up and down waiting for the arrival of the new car. This was due to be homologated in April 2003 and delivered to us in time for the Cyprus Rally in June. As further evidence of their total commitment, Subaru and

Prodrive agreed to lend us two of the current cars for the earlier Swedish and New Zealand events. And we duly got our campaign off to a fantastic start with Stig and Ana winning and Martin and Trevor Agnew coming 3rd in Sweden.

While the attempt to lift the Production Cup is obviously our main priority going into the 2003 season, the special 50th Anniversary Safari Rally promises a really exciting finish to the year. It was in honour of the Queen's Coronation that what later became known as the East African Safari and then simply the Safari was launched as the Coronation Rally in 1953 and the announcement of the anniversary event immediately sparked a fantastic response from drivers wanting to take part, including some of the most legendary names of all time.

We very quickly found ourselves with five confirmed entries, including a Skoda and four Escorts, one of them driven by Michele Mouton, with Ana Goni as her co-driver. At the same time, Hannu Mikkola, Markku Alen and Juha Kankkunen were among those actively looking for sponsorship and hoping to take part.

So, there is much to look forward to in the immediate future. As for the longer term, there's a villa in Spain where I keep promising Jill that she and I will soon be able to spend a little more time relaxing in the sun. But not just yet, it seems. At the time of writing, we are leading the World Championship in Group N and I can't help thinking to myself: "Here we go again!"

APPENDICES:

DRIVERS, CO-DRIVERS AND MECHANICS

THE DRIVERS

Five World Rally Champions have driven for me at various times over the last thirty years. The full list of drivers with whom I have been associated during that period is so long that this section alone would probably be worth a book in its own right. The names of most of them are listed at the end of this section, but if I happen to have missed anyone, I apologise. Those whom I have singled out for special mention below are the ones who have played leading roles in the story of my life.

Hannu Mikkola.

Unfortunately, I cannot claim Hannu as my own World Champion. That honour goes to Audi Sport. After my first casual meeting with him and his then best friend Timo Mäkinen in Sloane Square in 1968, I didn't really get to know Hannu until his Toyota British Championship days. Although fiercely competitive, he still had a reputation at that time as a hard drinking, heavy smoking party guy. I remember standing at the finish control at the end of a special stage on the Castrol Rally in Wales, then traditionally the last round of the British Championship, as Hannu arrived at an unholy speed. I then watched in amazement as he got out of the car and proceeded to pour what seemed like half-a-gallon of water out of his crash helmet. He was always known to sweat a lot, but I had never before seen anything quite like that. It was at that moment apparently that he resolved to give up the fags and the booze for good and he has never touched or drop or taken a drag from that day to this.

We first worked together when Ford Boreham prepared an

Eaton Yale Escort for us to manage and service on the Welsh Rally. This caused quite a problem at the time because the mechanics at Boreham were far from happy about preparing cars for outsiders like us to service and look after. The same awkwardness arose on several occasions, not just with us but with other Teams as well. In our case, we eventually arrived at a compromise whereby Boreham sent two mechanics along to assist us and keep an eye on the car.

Hannu and I have won many, many rallies together but the two most memorable victories as far as I am concerned were the 1978 RAC Rally, after I had been offered the chance to prepare his Escort at the time of the Ford strike, and the London-Mexico anniversary marathon in 1995, both of which, in different ways, had a significant effect on my fortunes.

When Hannu's first son, Juha, was born, it was a great honour for Jill and I to be invited to become godparents. This sealed a close friendship that I greatly value and that has now lasted 35 years.

Ari Vatanen

Ari is undoubtedly one of the most colourful characters in the whole of rally history. I think I can say without reservation that he has literally been everywhere, done everything and won everything, hit everything and crashed everything. I wonder if his consumption of body shells is more than Colin McRae's?!

I remember Peter Ashcroft saying to me on the 1000 Lakes Rally, after Ari had been guilty of yet another misdemeanour: "I really have got to sack him again!" When Ari and I later counted up his total number of sackings by Ford – both actual and threatened – they totalled seventeen. Nevertheless, he has a wicked sense of humour, was capable of the sort of speed that, in the early eighties, was unmatched by anyone and posseses a command of the English language and its idioms beyond any other Finn that I have ever come across.

With his strong religious beliefs he wouldn't tolerate swearing by the mechanics and yet had little respect for Team discipline and punctuality. I recall one occasion when the entire Rothmans Team was summoned to a publicity photo call and everybody turned up on time except Ari, of whom there was no sign. We all stood around in the windswept car park for about half-an-hour, glancing impatiently at our watches as we waited in vain for his arrival. Hannu was also in the Team and he eventually jumped into his car and, with a screech of tyres, drove back to the hotel, returning with a very sheepish and apologetic Ari.

On another occasion in the Canaries, Mike Pavitt, the Rothmans Public Relations Manager, went to great efforts to organise a press conference for the Team. Rothmans were as demanding as they were generous and the dress code on these formal occasions always involved official team blazers and ties, but Ari turned up looking extremely casual, not to say dead scruffy. Mike Pavitt took one horrified look and then gave him a ticking off that has stuck in my memory. "You look as if you've just been dressed by Oxfam," he said. "Leave the room and come back in your correct attire". Ari hung his head and shuffled off very meekly, like a naughty schoolboy.

His record consumption of Ford body shells stands to this day and, almost inevitably, he ended up having a horrific crash in Argentina from which he was very lucky to come out alive. He still looks about 25 years old, with a lock of blond hair falling across his forehead, but has mellowed sufficiently since his retirement from rallying to become a Finnish Member of the European Parliament.

Bjorn Waldegard

Bjorn is a giant of a man in terms of both personality and talent. He only drove for me on two occasions but it was a very pleasurable experience indeed. I endorse the old saying that was created at Ford – "With Waldegard's luck and Mikkola's speed, you could win every rally in the world."

Stig Blomqvist

Stig is quite the most pleasant and affable Swede I have ever met. He is a man of enormous talent and very few words and despite annihilating the opposition in virtually every event of the British Championship in 1983, during which he gave me my second RAC victory, I still felt at the end of the year that we hardly knew each other. He would arrive at service points and give his usual one word answer. "Is the car OK?". "Yes". "Do you want anything?". "No". Stig performed in that way for the whole year. Eighteen years later we rather unexpectedly renewed our relationship when he teamed up with Ana Goni in Group N. At 57, he remains as competitive as ever – although these days he has a little bit more to say for himself!

In his prime he loved to party and on one famous occasion he had to be dragged from a disco at four o'clock in the morning on the opening day of the RAC Rally, which he then went out and won by a massive margin.

Walter Rohrl

Walter, in my experience, is not at all the fearsome ogre and troublesome driver that he is sometimes accused being. I think he may sometimes be guilty of making unwise statements to the press, but, as a driver, he must rate as one of the greatest of all time, whether it be in the mountains of Monte Carlo, the snow of Sweden or the gravel roads of Portugal and Greece.

At the time he drove for Audi Sport UK, we were basically assisting the Factory with a testing programme for the newly arrived Audi Sport Quattro and as this had to include an event with some tarmac special stages we had entered the Ulster Rally. Walter and the awesome 550 bhp Sport Quattro duly obliterated the opposition and during the event we forged a very good understanding, with him regularly consulting me throughout about tactics and tyres. I had absolutely no problem with him at all and formed the opinion that with good, strong, intelligent handling, he was the kind of driver that any Team manager would want in his Team.

Gabriel Pozzo

As I have mentioned elsewhere, I am convinced that this young man - World Rally Champion in Group N at just 22 – has the potential to go on to even bigger and better things. The reason I was unable to find him a berth with one of the Factory teams was largely a matter of timing. His chance will come. Watch this space!

* * *

Markku Alen

Markku very much deserves to have been a World Champion and it is only really through bad luck that the title has eluded him. In 1986 he did actually hold it for 11 days until Peugeot's earlier disqualification was rescinded and he was relegated back to 2nd. His energetic, flamboyant style is very entertaining but, at the same time, his commitment is absolutely 100%.

I can proudly claim to have given him his first two drives outside his native Finland and, but for a minor slip in Sutton

Park on the 1973 Lombard RAC Rally, he would have caused a sensation by winning the event at his first attempt. I was unable to hang on to him simply because he was too expensive and too good for my little Team, so I handed him to Ford on a plate. He had two drives for them, one on the Arctic Rally and one on the Welsh Rally, which he won convincingly. However, as Ford had a full complement of drivers at that time, they couldn't offer him a permanent position either and so he was then snapped up by the Fiat Lancia Group, where he stayed until his retirement. It is interesting to note that the co-driver he took with him on the RAC Rally that he did for me, simply because he could speak English, remained with him for nearly twenty years, to my knowledge the longest-lasting relationship between a driver and co-driver in rallying history. Heaven only knows what they found to talk about!

Pentti Airikkala

Pentti came to England to find fame and fortune in much the same way as Markku. Affable and amusing, his great sense of humour meant that the rallies we did together were always a lot of fun. Pentti always drove for nothing and even paid his own expenses to get himself to and from England. All he wanted was the opportunity to win rallies in a good, competitive British-built car. It pains me to admit that he would almost certainly have won the RAC Rally in 1976 but for a poor decision on my part.Later, against all the odds, he also came within a mere 51 seconds of winning the 1000 Lakes.

Having made a name for himself, Pentti left me to join Vauxhall, where he had some considerable success. However, I think it was at this point that his life and personality started to change dramatically. He became rather conceited, telling anyone who cared to listen that he was the best rally test driver in the world, which, let me assure you, he never was! He also began to irritate everyone around him by regularly trying to change the specification of cars that had already been tried and tested by better and more experienced drivers. I wonder if he knew how many times it happened that after he had demanded rear shock absorbers to be changed, the mechanics would simply wash them, clean them and refit them to the rally car.

I did, nevertheless, respect him for his speed and experience, which is why I asked him back to join the Rothmans team in a third car in 1981. And, as you will have read earlier, he might easily have gone on to win the European Championship that same year if Rothmans had not thought otherwise, declining to give him a full programme after he had made a flying start.

Rauno Aaltonen

Rauno could possibly claim to be the original Flying Finn, although fans of Timo Mäkinen may disagree. It is already a matter of record that Rauno drove my Ford Escort on the 1970 London to Mexico and finished in a fantastic 3rd place overall and that with a little more information from Ford, the result may have been very different. I was always impressed by his charming manner, which, along with his word perfect command of the English language made him very easy to work with.

Saeed Al Hajri

The best of the Middle Eastern drivers, Saeed Al Hajri was Rothmans' property for more than ten years, ending up with an incredible list of successes to his name, not only in the Middle East but elsewhere around the world. I helped him to realise his ambition to become the first Arab driver to win an international event outside the Middle East, which he did when he won the Cork Rally in our Sierra Cosworth. Although Saeed didn't always keep himself in the best physical condition and seemed to break all the usual religious rules governing the lives of most Arabs, he was nevertheless a very formidable performer.

Roger Clark

What can I say about Roger that has not already appeared in every book and every magazine related to rallying in this country? He was the British driver that we all set out to emulate, his achievements unmatched until quite recently. It really does seem to be quite beyond belief that since Roger won his last World Championship event, it took 17 years for another British driver to equal this success. It was my pleasure to give him his last-ever international rally victory in Cyprus in 1980. Friends for many years, we were brought closer through suffering similar business problems, giving each other morale support. Sadly, he passed away in January 1998.

David Llewellin

When David first joined me at Audi Sport along with Michele Mouton, he was our third choice to drive the second car, both Mark Lovell and Louise Aitken-Walker having turned us down. But it didn't take me long to realise that they had done us a favour by opening the way for David to come in. One of the nicest and easiest drivers to work with, he won both the Scottish Rally and Cyprus Rally with us and my only surprise is that he didn't go on to make a name for himself at the highest level. A Works driver at various times with Austin Rover, Toyota, Nissan and Vauxhall, he twice won the British Championship with Toyota and yet a World Championship programme always somehow eluded him. Perhaps he lacked that little edge of ambition, or it could be that he needed a strong manager to develop his career. Maybe he was just unlucky. I tried very hard to find a place for him in the Ford Team, but Stuart Turner had clearly blackballed him because of three spectacular accidents, all of which unfortunately had been caught on film and were endlessly shown on television and used in videos. This was very unfair because David was never a particularly accident-prone driver. Whatever the reason, he was never quite able to fulfil his potential and has now retired back to his farm in Wales, happy to be able to devote more time to his young family.

Timo Mäkinen

No story connected with my work would be complete without a special mention of another flying Finn. Although we only worked together on two occasions, we have been friends for nearly 30 years. Even to this day, whenever Timo has the opportunity to drive his beloved Mini Coopers on historic events, he still gives a 100% performance. He is not always the easiest driver to work with and has some very fixed ideas, particularly about wheels and tyres, but he is, nevertheless, a good friend and a great competitor.

Michele Mouton

Although we had a disastrous year together in the Audi Sport UK Team, Michele is a very fierce competitor, without doubt the greatest female rally driver of all time. I first got to know her on the San Remo Rally when she beat us in typically bullish fashion. Starting the last night section with a lead over us of around 30 seconds, she kept her cool to take overall victory while our car crashed into the Italian scenery in a valiant but vain attempt to overtake her. Since her retirement we have stayed in constant touch and we regularly send cars down to her annual Race of Champions in Gran Canaria, the celebrity event that is her one remaining connection with motorsport.

Malcolm Wilson

Although capable of producing a devastating performance on occasions, Malcolm, like David Llewellin, never quite lived up to his promise as a driver, managing only a couple of Top Three finishes in over 40 World Championship starts before retiring in favour of a role behind the scenes. In some ways there are certain parallels between our two careers in so far as he has gone from being a small private Team manager to being handed the management of the Ford World Rally Team. To date, as I take great delight in telling him at every opportunity, the simularities end here since he has yet to match my achievement in winning the World Championship for Ford, although he has come very close.

THE CO-DRIVERS

Few Team Managers would dispute that co-drivers can be the most difficult people to deal with. They are the ones usually seen in the darkest corners of restaurants, doing deals with rival manufacturers, Team Managers and sponsors. Of course, they always claim that they are doing deals on behalf of their drivers first and foremost and their own requirements are secondary. Let me assure you that from my experience this is not very often the case. But here are some of the better ones with whom I have had the opportunity of working during the past 10 or 15 years.

David Richards

The most talented of them all, in my opinion – and I'm not just saying that because of a friendship stretching back more than twenty years or because I happen to be back working with him at Prodrive again. Or even because he is the most powerful and important figure in World Rallying these days! I have written at length elsewhere about the qualities that I believe made him so exceptional as a co-driver, the same qualities that I believe have contributed to his enormous success since then. I remember saying to him years ago that I didn't think he would ever be entirely satisfied until he was running a successful Formula 1 team and I suspect that this is still very much an ambition. Apart from that, I can see him going on even further to become the next Bernie Ecclestone or the next Max Mosley – or, knowing him, both!

Phil Short

Phil first came to my notice when he was co-driver to the ex jockey and rallycross driver, John Taylor. At that time, we would find ourselves competing in separate teams, quite often in Ireland, where Phil used to spend most of his time repairing the Irish scenery that John had destroyed! When I offered him the opportunity to join the Rothmans Team to co-drive for Pentti Airikkala in 1981 it was his first professional engagement. At various times after that I arranged for him to co-drive for no less than three World Champions – Bjorn Waldegard on the Welsh Rally, Hannu Mikkola on the Scottish and Walter Rohrl on the RAC. He was a winner with both Bjorn and Hannu but suffered a massive accident with Walter. When David Llewellin joined me at Audi Sport UK, Phil was the obvious choice to partner him as co-driver, a dream team that I believe could have been a force to be reckoned with in the World Championship had they ever had the chance. Phil went on to become Team Manager to Toyota and Mitsubishi and then retired with much media hype before promptly joining the Ford Rally Team a few weeks later!

Arne Hertz

Best known as Hannu Mikkola's regular partner for 13 years, Arne has also partnered a host of other famous and successful drivers, winning just about every event in the calendar at some time or other. A great friend and a wonderfully colourful character, he knows all the best restaurants in the world, a list he has built up over his many years on the road. He also has a wicked and roving eye for the ladies. Elsewhere in the book you will see a dramatic picture of the two Rothmans Escorts that crashed on the same corner on the same stage in Portugal, actually landing on top of each other. This unlikely feat was repeated some twelve years later in Greece in an accident involving two Toyotas – and, by an amazing co-incidence Arne happened to be one of the co-drivers on both occasions.

Henry Liddon

No story concerning my life would be complete without a mention of one of the true gentlemen of rallying, who sadly lost his life in an air crash whilst working for Toyota on the Ivory Coast Rally in 1987. Henry was the co-driver when Rauno Aaltonen drove my Escort to 3rd place in the original London-Mexico marathon back in 1970 and was also responsible for introducing Markku Alen into international and world class rallies.

He won an event with the talented Mike Hibbert, another driver who should have gone on to greater things, and was also a co-driver to Ari Vatanen on their victorious visit to Madeira. His passing was mourned by the entire rallying community and he remains sadly missed to this day. I am proud to have had the opportunity of working with such a fine man.

Fred Gallagher

Fred is not one of my most favourite people. I do not deny that he is talented, because as far as pure co-driving is concerned, his ability is second to none. I offered him a drive in the Rothmans Team with Saeed Al Hajri, but because of an existing commitment to Toyota, he was unable to join the Team until the April. This is quite unusual since most driver and co-driver contracts run from January to December. But because I felt that he had a value to us, I arranged for someone else to stand in for Fred for the first two events.

Later, when the Rothmans programme came to an abrupt halt due to the Gulf War crisis, we were all made redundant overnight. My Team was in chaos and as I have said earlier, our equipment was dotted all over the world. At the same time, the money supply from Rothmans was cut off immediately. I had no doubt whatsoever that as soon as Rothmans could recover from the disaster of having most of their offices closed, they would treat us fairly, but that we would have to be patient. Despite the fact that he had only done a couple of events for us at that stage, Fred decided that he wasn't prepared to wait and decided to take legal action against me to recover the fees which were due to him. Of course, he was paid in full and he has the singular distinction of having received a full year's co-driving fees for about 18 days work. I hope I am never again placed in a position where I have to consider him for a project that I may be involved in. I was particularly saddened by his attitude because we had won the Cyprus Rally some years earlier with John Buffum and I had always held his ability in high regard.

Pauline Gullick.

Pauline has been associated with us ever since the earliest days of David Sutton Cars Ltd. Jill and I first met her in the late sixties, when she was navigating for Rosemary Smith in the old

221

Motoring News Championship. She became Jill's co-driver in the mid-seventies and, together, they enjoyed great success and had a lot of fun in events all around the world. Later, she drove with both Pentti Airikkala and Michele Mouton at various times before going on to become John Lloyd's co-driver and then his full-time co-ordinator. Pauline worked for the Prison Service for many years, and has had to put up with being the butt of some very corny jokes as a result.

Gunnar Palm

My only direct involvement with Gunnar was when he came out of retirement to accompany Hannu in the 1995 anniversary re-run of the original 1970 London-Mexico. By then he had been out of rallying for twenty-three years but slipped back into the old routine as if he'd never been away. One of the legendary all-time greats, he is also a totally charming character and I was left wishing that I had had the opportunity to work with him more often.

THE MECHANICS

No publication about rallying would be complete without a word or two about the unsung heroes who work day and night and all through the weekend to get cars ready on time and then all round the clock to keep them competitive on the event itself, sometimes in appalling conditions. Lying under a rally car in the snow and mud in the middle of the night is all part of a day's work as far as they are concerned.

Wives and girlfriends are often a complication as far as globetrotting mechanics are concerned, since they soon get fed up with regular and prolonged absences. In this respect, the worst sort of mechanic is a single guy in love! The girlfriend is likely to be constantly on the phone, whingeing about the fact that he's not around to take her out on her birthday or the anniversary of their first date and then he's distracted and no longer able to concentrate on the job. With married men it can go either way. If there's trouble at home they either want to be excused foreign duties so that they can patch things up or they beg to be sent away at every opportunity so that they can avoid all the trouble and strife!

In recent years, some of the top mechanics have become superstars in their own right and I regard this as an unhealthy development. It can lead to some drivers forming a special relationship with a particular mechanic, as a result of which they can often be seen in a corner secretly discussing the specification of the car for the next event, while the Team management are left in the dark. For exactly this reason I made a point in my Rothmans and Audi days of never telling my drivers who exactly had prepared their car until after the event. I think the idea of a specific driver/mechanic partnership started at Ford, where Roger Clark built up a relationship with first Norman Masters and then Mick Jones, who actually became the subject of a television programme in his own right. One very real danger of letting a particular mechanic build a special car for a driver is that if the rally car encounters a problem at a service point and the mechanic who built it is not there, then the rest of the Team may have difficulty in finding the problem and rectifying it quickly.

John O'Connor

When I first took over Supersport from Rod Cooper in 1975, I inherited John O'Connor who is still with me to this day, nearly thirty years later. As I've said elsewhere in the book, John, in my opinion, is quite simply the best rally mechanic around. Not only can he build a fine car in the workshop, he can also work miracles at the roadside if the car has a problem. He was one of a group of mechanics who hold the world record for changing a Quattro gearbox in about 14 minutes, with every second of the operation recorded by a film team who happened to be on the spot. Quite understandably, John is happier these days with the Historic cars than the modern models with their complex electrical systems.

Ron Lumley

Ron drifted down to London from Newcastle and joined me at Clarke & Simpson, where he built some of the best Escorts that ever competed. Ron was also largely responsible for training John O'Connor. The ultimate perfectionist, it was said of him that if he was given a bodyshell in January and asked to have a car ready in time for the RAC Rally some eleven months later, he would still be carrying out final adjustments at scrutineering! I was saddened when, for family reasons, he could not relocate with us to Daventry and he will always have a special place in my memory.

World Champions, European Champions, National Champions, Clients, members of my family and other enthusiasts have all driven rally cars prepared by me. If my memory has failed and your name is not on the list, please accept my apologies.

A
Aaby, Erik
Aaltonen, Rauno
Aho, Kalevi
Airikkala, Penti
Al Hajri, Saeed
Al Marri, Jabber
Alen, Markku
Armstrong, Barbara

B
Blomqvist, Stig
Barbour, George
Barras, Etienne
Beever, George
Bennett, Brian
Beynon, Chris
Bin Sulayem, Mohammed
Bosch, John
Bostanci, Serdar
Buffum, John

C
Carello, Tony
Carter, Alan
Cinotto, Michele
Clark, Roger
Clark, Matthew
Clark, Oliver

Close, Russell
Coleman, Billy
Collinge, Rob
Corns, Mike
Cowan, Andrew
Cullen, James

D
Davis, Steve
Davison, Simon
De Vitta, Domingo
Demuth, Harald

E
East, Bob
Enomaa, Heikki
Eriksson, Kenneth

F
Fernandez, Beni

G
Gallagher, Drew
Goni, Ana
Guy, Callum

H
Hammonds, Tom
Hettema, Jan
Hibbert, Mike
Hudson, Ron

I
'Iaveris'

J
Johansson, Matt

K
Khayat, Mamdouh
Kleint, Jochi
Kochibay, Renc
Kullang, Anders

L
Laine, Antero
Lampi, Lasse
Lampinen, Simo
Lang, David
Lee, Barry
Lepley, Graham
Lezama, Fernando
Lindholm, Sebastian
Llewellin, David

M
Mikkola, Hannu
Maclean, Rod
Makinen, Timo
Maslen, Tony
McRae, Jimmy
Millen, Rod
Mouton, Michele

N
Nelson, Brian

O
O'Connor, John
Oliveira, Fernando
Oliveras, Bilo

P
Pozzo, Gabriel
Peres, Carlos
Phillips, Robin
Preston, Vic

R
Rohrl, Walter
Recalde, Jorge
Risso, Hector
Robinson, Guy
Robinson, Jill
Rowe, Martin

S
Samson, Charles
Savile, Sir Jimmy
Sclater, Chris
Sheppard, Toby
Simpson, Judy
Smith, Andrew
Sohlberg, Kari
Staepelaere, Gilbert
Sunsundegui, Ignacio

T
Tambay, Patrick
Taylor, John
Terzian, Vahan
Toivonen, Harri
Torres, Carlos
Tundo, Frank
Tuthill, Francis

V
Vatanen, Ari
Van der Merwe, Sarel
Vandervell, Colin
Vatanen, Tatu

W
Waldegaard, Bjorn
Weidner, Darryl
Whitney, Nick
Williams, Gareth
Wilson, Malcolm
Wise, Malcolm

THE LAST WORD

During the time this book was being compiled, quite a few friends, well wishers and other acquaintances got to hear about it. Almost everyone who knows me is expecting it to be filled with adulterous and sexual revelations, and other scandalous happenings.

Of course, I do have stories on just about everyone, including manufacturers, Team Managers, Drivers, Co-Drivers, Secretaries, Mechanics, Engineers, Sponsors and many others. If they were revealed, it would only bring unhappiness and embarrassment in the end.

Suffice it to say that I know who they are, and they know that I know who they are.

Perhaps in another book, sometime in the future ......